Nick Arley began his motorcycling journey at age eleven, and the open spaces of rural New South Wales fuelled what became a lifelong obsession.

Later in life Nick moved to Canberra taking up employment in the Federal Government. During the week it was all suits and ties, but speed and adventure were never far from his mind.

From competing in local offroad motorcycle events to riding across the Arctic Circle in Alaska, motorcycles have taken Nick far and wide. While living in Indonesia with his wife Nick regularly tested their Honda scooter to its limits exploring the offroad trails in Bali.

Returning home to Canberra, the desert started calling, Nick's rides became longer, evolving into multi-state odysseys crossing the country. The risks were as real as the danger, but these were the foundation for his greatest challenge: the fastest crossing of all ten Australian deserts unsupported on a motorcycle.

KING OF THE DESERT

ONE MAN'S WORLD-RECORD MOTORCYCLE CROSSING OF AUSTRALIA'S TEN DEADLY DESERTS

KING OF THE DESERT

NICK ARLEY

ALLEN&UNWIN
SYDNEY • MELBOURNE • AUCKLAND • LONDON

First published in 2025

Allen & Unwin
Cammeraygal Country
83 Alexander Street
Crows Nest NSW 2065
Australia
Phone: (61 2) 8425 0100
Email: info@allenandunwin.com
Web: www.allenandunwin.com

Allen & Unwin acknowledges the Traditional Owners of the Country on which we live and work. We pay our respects to all Aboriginal and Torres Strait Islander Elders, past and present.

EU Authorised Representative: Easy Access System Europe, Mustamäe tee 50, 10621 Tallinn, Estonia, gpsr.requests@easproject.com

NATIONAL LIBRARY OF AUSTRALIA
A catalogue record for this book is available from the National Library of Australia

ISBN 978 1 76147 233 6

Except where otherwise stated, all photographs are from the author's collection
Map by Guy Holt
Set in 12/18 pt Minion Pro by Midland Typesetters, Australia
Printed and bound in Australia by the Opus Group

10 9 8 7 6 5 4 3 2 1

MIX
Paper | Supporting responsible forestry
FSC® C001695
FSC www.fsc.org

The paper in this book is FSC® certified. FSC® promotes environmentally responsible, socially beneficial and economically viable management of the world's forests.

For Stace

Contents

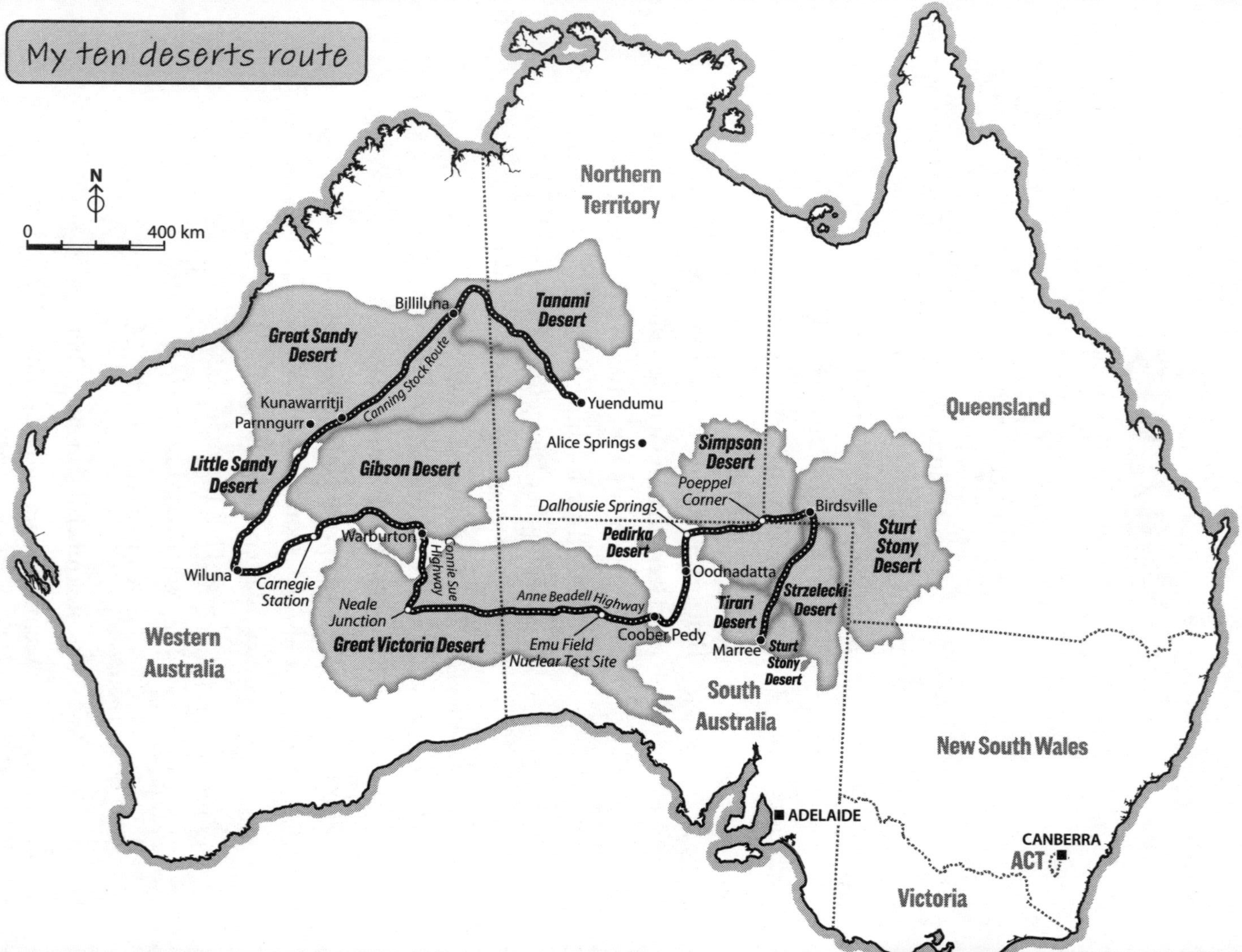

My ten deserts route
N
0
400 km
Northern Territory
Queensland
Western Australia
South Australia
New South Wales
Victoria
ACT
CANBERRA
ADELAIDE
Great Sandy Desert
Little Sandy Desert
Gibson Desert
Tanami Desert
Great Victoria Desert
Simpson Desert
Pedirka Desert
Tirari Desert
Strzelecki Desert
Sturt Stony Desert
Sturt Stony Desert
Billiluna
Canning Stock Route
Kunawarritji
Parnngurr
Wiluna
Carnegie Station
Warburton
Connie Sue Highway
Neale Junction
Anne Beadell Highway
Emu Field Nuclear Test Site
Coober Pedy
Oodnadatta
Dalhousie Springs
Poeppel Corner
Birdsville
Marree
Yuendumu
Alice Springs

Preface

My name is Nick Arley and I'm a 55-year-old guy who grew up in rural New South Wales and these days I live in Canberra, ACT. All my life I've ridden and owned dirt bikes and road bikes. They're a big part of my life—I guess you could say they're an obsession. My wife would certainly agree!

I live and breathe motorcycling. When I'm on a bike, it gives me a feeling of freedom a car can't provide. I feel part of the environment I'm travelling through, I see the sights clearer, smell the smells better and hear the sounds as they become part of me. Motorcycling also allows me to forget the daily stresses and strains of life. When I ride, I feel a real sense of focus. I just want to keep riding, eating up the miles, seeing new things, not stopping. I'm sure other riders can relate.

I've ridden or owned all different types of bikes, from minibikes when I was young, to motocross bikes, enduro bikes, road bikes, and large and small adventure bikes. I find the adventure bikes suit what I like to do best, which is exploring and travelling off-road. Their versatility and do-anything design allows me to get out there and do whatever I want to do.

I wrote this book to document a fantastic motorcycling experience I had in 2023, when I beat the Guinness World Record for 'The Fastest Time to Cross All Ten Australian Deserts on Motorbike', riding solo and unsupported. I want to share not only the details of the ride itself—and it was certainly an emotional roller-coaster, with some serious highs and lows along the way—but also what I learned along the way about the unique challenges and joys of outback riding.

1

Passion

My love of dirt bikes and long-distance riding started way back.

I was born in England and migrated to Australia as a five-year-old boy with my mum and grandparents, joining my aunty who was already living here. Mum and I first settled in Sydney, like many other immigrants do, however the rat race soon had Mum looking for a better life outside the urban environment. She was a horsey person, so after a couple of years she, my grandparents and I moved to a small country town called Bribbaree, in the Riverina area of New South Wales.

The 1980s was a great time to be a kid, especially in a village with a population of fewer than 100 people. There was also the town emu, which I remember as a feathery beast that would roam the main street and school playground, seeking out small children whose lunch it could steal. On more than one occasion it managed to get my devon and tomato sauce sandwich!

Back then there was no internet and mobile phones hadn't yet become a thing. It was a much simpler time, when you had to make your own fun. In a rural village, that fun often involved motorcycles or old cars—paddock bashers, as we called them—as well as camping, all good outdoorsy stuff which I loved. The fact that there was no police station in our town probably helped me and the other kids develop our riding and driving skills well before we were legally old enough!

Like Mum, I was into horses. We had several horses which were used for showing, cross-country jumping and sporting events. I began competing in these events at the local shows and gymkhanas, which was fun at the time, but the horses required a fair bit of effort to maintain. We branched out into breaking in horses and training them, and I often had the honour of being the first to sit on a horse's back—and of course of being the first to get bucked off! I rode everything from 16-hand thoroughbreds to small ponies, which were both equally challenging.

I was once breaking in a small brown pony, and the day had come when I would ride it for the first time. It was so small that the girth strap we had was a bit too big, and after I got on and it started bucking and prancing around, the saddle slipped underneath its belly—me included! I was on the ground beneath the horse, dodging kicking legs and scrambling out of the way. That got me thinking of other pastimes that might be easier. Feeding, watering, mucking out stables and grooming, along with getting bucked off, was getting a bit tiresome.

My very first ride on a motorbike was on a white Honda Z50, and I remember that bike to this day. It was owned by Leigh-Ann, a girl I went to school with. Her father had bought it for her to ride around the nearby cricket oval. She only brought it out on weekends, and it was immaculate. Shiny chrome wheels and handlebars, a white tank with the yellow winged Honda badge, and black seat cover—it really caught my attention.

One weekend, I was riding my BMX bike and I saw her with her Z50 at the oval, so I rode over to say hello. We chatted for a while before I gathered up the courage to ask her for a ride. To my surprise, she agreed. I remember jumping on this bike and thinking how small it was—the wheels were smaller than those of my BMX—but it also had a very different feel to it, with the weight of a motor. She showed me the controls, which were pretty simple: right hand on the throttle, twist and go, front brake on the handlebars, rear brake on the foot pedal, and the gear lever on the left. 'Okay,' I said, and off I went.

Wow! The feeling of riding around that cricket oval without pedalling was unreal. I was hooked and we spent an hour together, doing laps around the cricket pitch. This little bike instantly opened up a new world for me, and my obsession with motorcycles began. Riding my BMX was never the same again.

Around the same time, another of my school buddies had been given a Yamaha YZ80G. It was yellow, loud and blew blue smoke everywhere. I'd only read about motocross bikes in magazines, so this was the first one I'd seen in real life. This was a racing machine, and so much cooler than a Honda Z50!

My friend used to ride around a paddock close to his house, and he took me for a double on the back one day. After I pestered him for a couple of weeks, he eventually let me have a ride. With only my half-hour's riding experience on the Z50, I thought the YZ80G was a weapon! It had a clutch, which meant you had to rev the engine and let the clutch out to go. I had never used a clutch before, and I wasn't aware of the narrow power bands of the peaky two-stroke motocross bikes of the time. But the pressure was on me not to stall it or fall off in front of my mate.

I revved the engine a bit and slowly let the clutch out as instructed, and moved off. At first it felt quite sluggish, but he had told me to rev it more before changing up through the gears. When I hit the power band, this little thing shot ahead, screaming its head off, and suddenly it was going faster than anything I had felt before.

The adrenaline rush was instant—I could hear the noise of the two-stroke motor screaming and smell the classic blue smoke coming out of the exhaust. It was addictive—I had to have one.

Not long after that, I gave up competing on the horses, much to Mum's disappointment, and pestered my family for a motorbike.

And for my twelfth birthday, my granddad bought me a second-hand yellow Suzuki TC125.

What I didn't know at the time was that the TC125 was basically an agricultural or 'ag' bike, with high and low range and auto oil injection. I modified it to try to make it look more like a motocross machine, adding a front numberplate, removing all the road-going gear and of course taking out the baffles!

My mate's YZ80G was still faster than it, but I didn't care—I loved my bike. It was my freedom machine, and I rode that thing to death. I learned how to replace the piston and rings, how to file the points when it started running a little rough, how to clean an air filter and pull apart a carburettor. As a kid, I wasn't very consistent in doing these things, but that bike taught me the basics of motorcycle maintenance. This stood me in good stead later in life when I wanted to tinker with and maintain my other bikes.

•

After I left school in 1986, I moved to Canberra, where most of my schoolmates had gone. It was a natural progression for kids in my area who didn't want to stay and work on a farm or in a small town. My motorbiking career got put on hold for a few years as partying took precedence.

I re-entered the bike scene in the early 1990s on a series of Honda XRs—they were the bikes to have back then. I started off on an XR250RN, which I had bought brand-new. I was keen to try my hand at competing in some of the local motorcycle races on my new bike, and soon joined the local motorcycle club in Canberra.

'Pony Express' events were popular at the time, and I wanted to give them a go. A Pony Express was a cross-country race, and locally they were usually held in one of Canberra's pine forests, with a mixture of single-track riding and open fire trails. They're an endurance event of varying length, but usually at least four hours' duration. They contained several classes, which catered for all capacity bikes and rider skill levels, and could be ridden as a team event with two riders, or solo as an 'Ironman'. I chose Ironman, and had to complete the entire race myself, which was a real effort.

To ready my little XR for competition, I removed the restrictor plates in the carburettor intake. That was an easy modification to make and probably increased the power a little. It was the simplest performance mod you could do, but otherwise it was bog stock. I flogged the life out of it, winning a few trophies along the way.

This was also the bike I started using to explore Canberra and its surrounds. There is plenty of bushland around the national capital, and the Brindabella Ranges became familiar riding territory. Every winter it snows up on the higher peaks, and I rode the little XR there many times, exploring new trails.

It wasn't too long before I felt the need for more. Back then I thought more horsepower would make me faster—how wrong I was. I sold the XR250RN and found a highly modified XR600RM. This thing was a beast, and had more modifications than any other bike I'd owned. It had a set of upside down or 'inverted' front forks from a Honda CR500 motocross bike. This was a big upgrade to the front suspension from the XR's conventional front end. The motor was bored out to 654cc to increase the capacity, which increased its output, and it was fitted with a performance 42mm flat-slide carburettor that delivered more fuel which equalled more power.

Oversize cooling fins were added to the motor to cope with the increased heat that more power created, along with a larger performance exhaust system that consisted of a Muzzy header pipe, and SuperTrapp exhaust pipe. The rear shock absorber had also been upgraded with a heavy-duty rear spring and the seat had been raised slightly with firmer foam which was hard as a rock. The motor had a fairly high compression ratio for the time of 12:1 and trying to start that bike without breaking a leg was quite a job.

I took my new XR out to the next Pony Express, believing I'd smoke the competition. At that time, European manufacturer Husqvarna had the fastest off-road big-bore bike with the TE 610 enduro. This had the most power and speed and was the one to beat. But I thought I stood a good chance against it on my new bike.

It was a Le Mans–style start: you stand facing your bike with the front wheel between your legs. The starter drops the flag and you run around the side of your bike, jump on and kick-start it. Electric starters weren't yet commonplace, so you needed good technique with your right leg. I had the kick-starter primed on top dead centre with the bike warmed up, hoping it would fire up on the first kick.

The flag dropped and I ran around the side of the bike, jumping on with one movement down on the kick-starter, and the bike roared into life. I dumped the clutch and gave it full throttle, and this thing took off like a rocket. I smoked the entire field off the start, including a couple of Husky 610s—I was pumped!

I led the field at the first corner, heading onto the single track in the forest. I was riding my hardest, and that was where it all came undone. The bike was performing faultlessly, and blisteringly fast.

It handled the terrain easily, my fitness however was no match for this machine. The bike was pulling like a freight train, so hard that my arms began to pump up with my forearm muscles swelling from the intense riding, making it hard to hold the handlebars. Then the cramping came in, followed by the exhaustion. I was in bad shape, and this bike was letting me know it. I finished the event but didn't place, as I was knackered. Sometimes more isn't always better: I realised I was actually faster on my smaller XR250!

•

It was around this time that I tried my hand at touring on the XR600, with a ride from Canberra to the small town of Texas, in Queensland, riding as much dirt as I could find. This was the longest off-road adventure ride I'd done, long before the terms 'adventure riding' and 'adventure bikes' had even been coined. The only problem was that the big XR had been set up for racing: it had very hard suspension, no windscreen, little in the way of luggage capacity and a rock-hard seat. There were no specialised products for the adventure touring market at this time, so people just made do with what they could build or use from the road bike sector.

I found a set of soft panniers that I threw over the seat, and bought a small biker swag with a paper-thin foam mattress and sleeping bag. I was young, keen and set! My route took me on back roads through Forbes, Parkes, Nyngan and Lightning Ridge, places that seemed so far away.

That trip gave me my first sense of escapism in the outback of western New South Wales—it was awesome. I felt like a real explorer and loved every minute of it. Every new dirt road, small country town and change of scenery enthralled me. Even though my swag was cold and uncomfortable and my panniers melted on the bike's exhaust, I wanted more. I just loved it. It sparked my passion for the outback, which continues to this day.

Not long after, I gave away the dirt bikes and moved into road bikes. The lure of powerful bikes attracted me, and I'd never owned a big road bike so I wanted to try them. My first road bike was a red, white and blue Honda CBR1000F. It was a heavy, long and stable bike. Very comfy and fast for long-distance riding, but not very agile. I rode that thing all over the place, but eventually upgraded to a Honda VFR800 purchased from a friend. The VFR was much lighter and more agile, and heaps of fun to wheelie! I really enjoyed that bike as well.

In time, that bike was sold for another Honda, a black VTR1000 Firestorm. That bike sounded awesome: with a set of Staintune exhausts, the V-twin roared. Not very practical for a six-foot, 100-kilogram bloke, even though it did make me feel like Mick Doohan!

After riding road bikes for eight or nine years, the bush and the dirt began calling me again. During my road bike years, I had also owned a couple of smaller dirt bikes, including a Suzuki RMX250, which I used to go mustering with a mate, Robbo, up in south-east Queensland each year. In 2006 Robbo and I headed off for our annual trip, but this time we decided to go a bit further afield to the Birdsville Races. To my mind, Birdsville was the holy grail of the outback. The mystique of the place was calling us both, so we drove there in Robbo's Toyota Prado.

There are a couple of ways you can get to Birdsville, but the most well-travelled is up through Windorah and along the Birdsville

Developmental Road. When the horse races are on, the traffic up that way gets quite busy, with all shapes and sizes of four-wheel drives and bikes making their way there. We were driving along the dirt section on the Developmental Road when Robbo said there were a couple of bikes coming up behind us. The road was all dirt, and about six car widths' wide. Not long after, I heard the roar of two V-twins catch us and cruise past.

I'd never seen anything like those bikes before. I had no idea what they were, but man, they looked cool. They looked like Paris–Dakar rally bikes and sounded like V8s! I said to Robbo that when we got to Birdsville, I was going to find those bikes and riders and discover what they were.

Not long after that, we got a flat tyre on the rocky dirt road and stopped to fix it. A bloke named Jim, who was driving a Mitsubishi L300 van, pulled over to see whether we needed any help. He was travelling solo with his blue heeler, Morton. We had a chat, fixed the flat and continued on to Birdsville.

That afternoon we arrived in Birdsville and set up camp on the common. With us was our new friend, Jim. The common is a flat, open expanse of grassland just out of town, where visitors during the races are allowed to camp. From there, it's just a short walk into town to go to the famous Birdsville Hotel for a beer, a chat and a feed. I rolled my swag out on the ground, little suspecting that Morton would claim it as his own and would be sharing it with me that night!

The next day I went for a walk around town and spotted one of the bikes I'd seen the day before being refuelled at a garage. I walked over and spoke to the owner, who told me it was a KTM 950 Adventure. I'd never seen anything like it. I was mesmerised by its size and shape, with those big side-by-side fuel tanks. It looked like a beast, and I knew then that this would be my next bike.

We had a great time at the races, making new friends and socialising. One of the highlights was Fred Brophy's boxing tent. I'd never seen anything like it before. Anyone can put their hand up for a boxing match against one of Brophy's fighters under the big top. It was all for entertainment and not taken too seriously—those who did were quickly put in their place by the trained boxers. Brophy's is the last boxing troupe of its kind in Australia. These were the sort of things you'd never see anywhere but in the outback, and the very reasons I wanted to explore it.

When I got home, my VTR was quickly sold, and then I began a quest to find my new bike. I researched the KTMs and decided I wanted one of the newer fuel-injected 990s with the long travel suspension. Eventually, I located a near-new one in Newcastle, which its original owner found too tall. Pretty soon a blue KTM 990 Adventure S was on my trailer and heading down the highway to Canberra. Purchasing this bike marked the beginning of my true outback exploring.

This was my first European bike, and I quickly became aware of the increased maintenance requirements. I also started adding 'farkles', or fancy accessories. First came a set of Wings exhaust pipes, panniers and rack, and a custom touring seat. It wasn't long before I was out exploring the Canberra region and the Victorian High Country.

Being at the foot of the New South Wales snowfields and the Kosciuszko National Park gave me endless opportunities to explore and camp in the wilderness. The country up there is pristine alpine wilderness, with wild brumbies roaming the plains.

Every chance I got, I would take my big KTM into this area to explore and camp.

Over the next few years, I expanded my off-road touring to Cape York, Central Australia and the Kimberley. I couldn't get enough of it. Pretty soon my love of exploring Australia's remote regions by motorcycle would see me setting bigger and bigger challenges for myself.

2

Glow in the Dark

It was 2022 and Covid-19 had been raging around the world for over two years, and I decided to go for a three-week desert ride with a mate. This was no ordinary ride, as it would set me up for the biggest challenge of my riding life.

The ride was to be a variation of one I'd planned but hadn't been able to undertake due to the dreaded Covid—a plan B, you might say. I had intended to ride the famous Canning Stock Route (CSR) solo and unsupported. The CSR runs south-west from Halls Creek, in the Northern Territory, through desert country for around 1850 kilometres, ending at Wiluna, Western Australia.

The adventure had been on my bucket list for years and I'd finally bought what I felt was the right bike, a Suzuki DR650. But the Western Australian government had kept its side of the country locked up. While the eastern states were mostly out of lockdown, Western Australia stubbornly refused to open its borders, and when it did, it still had in force a number of public health declarations that prohibited tourist travel into the remote Indigenous communities across the state, which included the communities along the CSR that I needed to enter. These communities included the townships of Parnngurr and Kunawarritji.

While I waited for Western Australia to open up, I started on a plan B ride just in case, and it too would be a very challenging ride. It would see me riding through six of Australia's ten deserts, in some very remote country. But I still held out hope that the CSR ride would be possible.

To make the adventure more interesting, I invited two of my buddies, Kurtis and 'Farmer', to join me. Kurtis had been a mate for a few years. We met through a work deployment in Afghanistan and realised we had a common interest in dirt bikes and remote travel. He'd ridden road bikes before moving on to dirt bikes, and had never looked back. We had ridden some gnarly tracks together in the Victorian High Country, so I knew he was solid.

Kurtis had a well set up DR650. To be honest, his bike probably had more farkles than the bike itself was worth, but it was well suited to a ride of this type.

Anthony Nicholls, or 'Farmer', as he's always been known to me, was a farmer—surprise, surprise! I met him years ago through another riding buddy. I'd ridden with Farmer many times on bigger bikes, me on my KTM 990 Adventure S and him on his BMW 1250 GS. He was also a capable and well-organised rider, and looked after his bikes.

For a remote ride like this, all riders need to be reliable, able to work on their own bikes, have meticulous preparation and organisational skills, and know how to ride safely and within their limits. Both Kurtis and Farmer fitted the bill exactly so I had no hesitation inviting them. For an adventure of this sort, it's essential to know your riding buddies well: you have to be able to trust each other.

One of the unwritten rules for a trip like this is the 'help and holiday' rule. If another rider breaks down, falls or otherwise has a mishap, the others must stop and render whatever assistance is necessary to ensure their mate is fully taken care of, whether that be repairing a bike, rendering first aid or waiting for the Flying Doctor after an emergency beacon activation. A 'team first' mentality is essential in the outback. Once the rider is cared for, the other riders should be free to complete the ride, as a lot of time, money and effort is spent arranging and taking big trips like this. We all agreed this was the way things would work.

Our departure date was set for 26 June 2022. As the day drew closer, however, Kurtis told Farmer and me that, because there had been a new addition to his young family, he had to withdraw from the ride. I was disappointed as I was looking forward to riding with him again, but Kurtis assured us he would keep an eye on our GPS trackers.

By this time, it was clear that I had to cancel my CSR ride, but Farmer and I agreed that plan B was definitely on. There was one problem, though: in Farmer's stable of bikes, he didn't have anything suitable for this type of trip. So he started scouring Gumtree and Facebook Marketplace with a vengeance, looking for a DR650. The year didn't really matter as the DRs haven't changed for ages—they're all the same, which is handy.

Not long after, there was a second-hand Suzuki DR650 sitting in Farmer's shed. It was equipped with a long-range fuel tank and pannier racks, which was a good start, and he got to work adding a few farkles he thought necessary.

We worked out our itinerary. First, we'd meet up in Wagga Wagga and ride about two thousand kilometres west across the continent to the Old Eyre Highway, in South Australia. We would follow it to the West Australian border, then north up to the Trans-Australian Railway line, and follow that west. From Rawlinna, we planned to turn north on the Connie Sue Highway, then onto the Anne Beadell Highway, Ilkurlka, continuing east all the way to Coober Pedy, before heading into the Simpson Desert and Madigan Line via Mount Dare. Once across the Simpson, we would head east from Birdsville, down to Innamincka, and back to Wagga Wagga via Ivanhoe, in western New South Wales.

We had plenty of logistics to sort out, including permits and fuel drops. I'd arranged most of mine already, and Farmer got busy emailing the various Aboriginal land councils and the Department of Defence to get permission to pass through government and Aboriginal lands. We also had to reserve some Opal fuel at the Ilkurlka Roadhouse, Australia's most isolated roadhouse, on the Anne Beadell Highway.

Once the planning was underway, time flew. Many a night was spent on the phone discussing what we needed to take, how to load the bikes, fuel ranges needed, water and camping supplies. Riding the same bikes make things a little easier, as we could share tools and didn't have to take two of everything. I like to take a book with me on trips like this, something to enjoy after a hard day's riding. The books are usually about the country I'm in or motorcycles. For this trip I'd packed what I thought was a story all about adventure motorcycling, and I was keen to get into it. Little did I know the impact it would have on me.

•

The desert riding season in Australia is during the winter months, as the temperatures are lower and it's safer to travel. Some of the deserts are closed during the summertime anyway, as temperatures regularly exceed 50 degrees Celsius. However, in Canberra , it's freezing during winter, which makes for uncomfortable riding. So we had to be warm enough to ride down south and yet not overheat in the desert.

On 26 June I set off on a typically freezing Canberra morning. The temperature was barely above zero by the time I arrived at the Wagga Wagga roadhouse and peeled my frozen body off the little DR. My hands were numb and my teeth were chattering. Farmer was already there, punctual as ever, so a hot cup of coffee inside the roadhouse was our first item of business. We talked excitedly about the trip ahead as we warmed up over the first of many roadhouse instant coffees.

The ride was fairly uneventful for the first three to four days, as we made our way across New South Wales, into Victoria and then South Australia. This was the easy part, all tar roads and pub stays. Even with the cold temperature, we knew that at the end of the day we'd be able to have a hot shower and a cold beer—what more could you want?

The fun began when we approached the Nullarbor Plain, where we had decided to take the Old Eyre Highway. This is the road that was used to travel east–west before the sealed section of the current Eyre Highway as we know it today was built. In some places the old road runs close to the new, while in others it takes you deep into the Nullarbor Plain, which has unique scenery.

We followed the Old Eyre Highway as long as we could to our planned overnight stop of Bunda Cliffs, on the Great Australian Bight. The track meanders along roughly parallel with the main highway, and as you near the Bunda Cliffs it divides into a cobweb of many smaller tracks that lead right to the edge of the Australian continent. We rode down one of them, hoping to get a look at the coastline, and were rewarded with an incredible view. The ruggedness of the coastline was awesome, and this—combined with the blustering winds at the time—gave a raw power to the place. It was exhilarating.

We had planned to camp there for the night but hadn't anticipated the severity of the wind, which would have ripped our lightweight tents to pieces if we were somehow able to get them up, so we decided to push on. The next settlement was Border Village, on the South Australian and Western Australian border, and we were lucky enough to get a room at the motel attached to the roadhouse for the night.

Once we had unpacked and cleaned up, we wandered across the dirt car park in the motel to the roadhouse bar for a couple of beers before dinner. It was still blowing a gale and starting to sprinkle rain, so I was pleased we had made the decision to ride on.

It wasn't long before we were joined by another rider, Peter, who was riding his KTM 1290 Super Adventure around Australia. He had left Perth a few days before and was travelling solo, mostly on the tar. He was loving the power and comfort of the big KTM and told us all about it while we swapped stories about our trips. Peter was impressed by our adventurous route but preferred the comforts of the big KTM and its ability to eat up the miles. On a trip like ours you meet so many like-minded and interesting people, which makes for fun times.

The next morning we were to make our way up to a small settlement called Forrest. It had rained overnight and the bikes were damp, which made me wonder just how much water would be on the dirt tracks we would be traversing. We had rung ahead and spoken to the caretaker at Forrest, who had assured us there was fuel available, but we each loaded up one of our 12-litre fuel bladders just in case. Along with the 36 litres in our fuel tanks, this gave our DRs a range of about 850 kilometres, which would be just enough to make it all the way to Ilkurlka without any refuelling stops if we had to. We changed out our front sprockets for smaller 14-tooth ones, which would better suit the slower speeds and dirt roads ahead.

The road up to Forrest was no more than a dirt track. It wasn't signposted and had multiple tracks going in all directions. Solid navigation was required to ensure we didn't head off into the bush and God knows where! The 150 kilometres to Forrest was slow going, as we wove and bounced along the unmaintained track, however the rain hadn't affected it too much. In fact, it had dampened the dust, making the conditions more pleasant.

Forrest is like a little oasis in the desert, with a small collection of buildings, a caretaker's house and an airstrip. It sits just north of the Trans-Australian Railway and has one caretaker to look after everything. Apparently, Forrest airport is a major refuelling point for light aircraft travelling across the Nullarbor, so the caretaker has to be a jack of all trades.

We rode north to the dead-straight tracks of the Trans-Australian Railway, pausing for a moment to see the lines running off to the horizon in both directions, Perth to the west and Sydney to the east. It felt very isolated. We looked for the most lived-in building in the small settlement, which turned out to be Mick's place.

Mick was the caretaker at Forrest. A Kiwi, he lived there with his wife; they'd been posted there for two years. Mick took us over to the aerodrome and opened up the fuel shed, where he filled up our bikes from 44-gallon drums. This was how the planes were fuelled up, Mick assured us, but still I worried whether this was clean fuel that wouldn't cause us any problems later on.

Mick invited us back to his house, and we sat down with him and his wife for a cuppa and a chat. They didn't get many visitors, so they took advantage of any travellers for a yarn. Mick regaled us with funny stories of all the weird and wonderful travellers he'd met over the past year or two when they stopped at Forrest for fuel.

We told him all about our trip, which would no doubt add to his repertoire for the next traveller. Before we knew it, an hour had passed, so we excused ourselves and were on our way again.

Now we headed due west, following the Trans-Australian Railway. Our dirt track was winding and very bumpy, so our maximum speed was just 40 to 50 kilometres an hour, for hours and hours. All I wanted to do was get into fourth gear and go, but the track just wouldn't open up. Because of this it was very hard to get into any sort of riding rhythm, and very tiring. We stopped every 50 kilometres or so where there was a communication tower or something similar, to have a break and stretch our legs.

It might not sound like much, but an hour of riding on heavily laden bikes on soft roads was physically demanding, so breaks were essential. During one of these stops, we heard a train approaching. Sure enough, it was a transcontinental train, the *Indian Pacific*, heading west. The driver sounded his horn as he passed us and gave us a wave. We waved and gave a beep on our bikes' horns but I doubt he heard it. He was probably wondering what these two mad blokes were doing out in the middle of nowhere!

Our goal that day was to make it to the Connie Sue Highway, but before we started the Connie Sue, we wanted to ride a little further into the town of Rawlinna. It's another town situated on the Trans-Australian Railway line and has its own railway station. But it's a ghost town and had an eerie feeling. We saw an odd collection of buildings and a machinery shed, but the place gave off real *Mad Max* vibes. We had a quick ride around as the sun was setting and saw no one, not even a stray dog. Time to get out of here! We back-tracked a little to a painted tractor tyre which marked the turnoff for the Connie Sue Highway.

We rode up the Connie Sue for a couple of kilometres before riding into the scrub and setting up our camp for the night. This was our first night of bush camping, so it was out with the tents and on with the 'bush telly'—that being a large fire to keep us warm and entertained. Our spirits were high. It was our first outback camp for the trip, our bikes were running well and we'd had an interesting day.

As I turned in after dinner, I had a chance to start reading my new book called *Hunting Fear* by Benji Brundin. Benji was the current Guinness World Record holder for the fastest time to cross all ten Australian deserts on a motorbike. I assumed the book would be all about motorbikes, adventure riding and his Guinness World Record, as the cover suggested, but it started off quite differently. Initially it delved into the author's life situation with little about adventure riding. Even so I committed to reading it.

The Connie Sue Highway is one of a network made by the Australian explorer and surveyor Len Beadell. Back in the 1950s Len made a series of roads in outback Australia, naming a number of them after his family: the Connie Sue Highway was named after his infant daughter at the time. Most of Len's roads are now unmaintained tracks, as we would soon discover.

After a great first camp, we hit the Connie Sue Highway the next day—only to find it was no highway at all, but rather kilometres of corrugations, sand dunes, deep sand and more corrugations.

Corrugations, or washboarding, describes when a dirt road develops a series of ripples or ridges, which get larger as more vehicles travel over them. On a maintained dirt road, a grader will be used to flatten them out again, but out here there was no chance of that happening. The ridges were up to 15 centimetres high.

They were extremely hazardous to ride on, and could easily cause you to lose control of your bike due to the severe vibrations they caused.

There were also sand dunes, which I hadn't anticipated at this point of the ride. These weren't as big as the dunes we would meet later, in the Simpson Desert, but I'd never encountered one before, and the first one had my heart pumping! Sure, I'd ridden sand before, but never a dune.

The first one was about six metres tall, and when I saw it I knew instantly that I had to power up and over it. I didn't have much time to react, so I just stood up, gassed it and hoped for the best. The bike went straight up, I held the power on going down, and I'd made it. Fortunately, there were only a few dozen of these dunes, but they gave us a taste of things to come.

We continued north and linked up to the Anne Beadell Highway, named after Len's wife. The Anne Beadell, much like the Connie Sue, was a corrugated and sandy track running for hundreds of kilometres. It was near an intersection called Neale Junction, and that was where we made our second night's camp.

As this was a major track junction—by outback standards, at least—there was a campsite not far off the track, with a small water tank (which was dry) and an aluminium shelter and picnic table. The ground was hard and I had difficulty driving in my lightweight tent pegs without bending them. This was also the first time on the trip I'd seen camel footprints showing where a herd had recently passed through.

Once we were set up, I walked up to Neale Junction and signed the visitors' book. These are common on outback tracks and places of interest, and travellers like to sign them and leave a few comments.

They're a good source of entertainment to see what earlier travellers have written and where they came from.

The next day would see us head east along the Anne Beadell. Again the riding was tiring: we were constantly scanning the terrain, changing lines and looking for hazards, which now included the humped variety. Our destination that night was to be Australia's most remote roadhouse, Ilkurlka. There we would meet Phil, who lives there with his three dogs, servicing the nearby Tjuntjuntjara community with fuel and basic food supplies. It also serves as an outlet for local Aboriginal art.

Farmer and I had decided to spoil ourselves and book the only donga. It's a small room with a pull-out bed, a fridge, a donkey shower and stove. A donkey shower is an old Australian bush shower consisting of a drum of some sort holding the water and a receptacle underneath for a fire. We got the fire going and about fifteen minutes later had hot water—a luxury after a couple of nights in the bush.

Phil was very hospitable, showing me around his private veggie patch providing some fresh tomatoes and capsicums for that night's cook-up, which also consisted of chicken drumsticks (which we'd purchased at great expense from the roadhouse) and potatoes. Farmer was able to show off his culinary skills and whipped up a lovely dinner.

When we'd stayed in hotels, Farmer and I had been alternating as to who got the larger bed, and tonight it was his turn. The only problem was that there was only one bed in the donga we had, so it was cushions on the floor for me. After a good feed, I had no trouble relaxing on the pillows and I read a few more pages of the book I'd brought along with me. Benji had been going through a difficult period in his life and was describing his story—still there was no mention of adventure bikes. I was somewhat confused. This wasn't the book I thought it was going to be.

•

The next morning we fuelled our bikes up out of 44-gallon drums again and continued east for Coober Pedy, which was about 800 kilometres away—with no settlements in between. This was the leg of the trip I was most excited about, as it would take us through the Emu Field.

In the 1950s, the British were looking for areas in which to test atomic weapons. The Australian government agreed to host them and employed Len Beadell to find a suitable site. He located a large claypan that was used as an airstrip to ferry men and supplies to the soon-to-be-growing village at Emu Field.

It took us two days of riding through sand dunes, corrugations and camels to reach Emu Field, which is about 270 kilometres west of Coober Pedy. On the second night we set up camp near the intersection of the road to Maralinga. There was a lot of excitement around the campfire that night as Farmer and I discussed how we would explore the test site.

Before dark, we walked up to the old village site, which overlooked the area of the atomic tests. The footings of old building were still visible in the ground, and we could see where there had been roadways. We also spotted old artefacts such as bottles and bits of metal frames from the houses.

I was up early the next day, ready to go exploring. We rode down to the old airstrip first, which was in pretty good shape.

The claypan was flat and long, so we just had to drag-race our fat DRs up and down a few times for the fun of it. There was a large amount of rusting metal lying around on the side of the airstrip: old tracks from the machinery used, an old windvane and numerous old drums that had just been abandoned. We spent about an hour riding around and taking pictures. I couldn't believe how much stuff had been left out there—it was everywhere.

The highlight was going to the totems that marked where the atomic bombs had been detonated. About 20 kilometres down the road from the airstrip were totems one and two. Warning signs were spread out in a line for kilometres, advising visitors not to camp or eat the wildlife due to the radiation. That got the hairs on my neck standing up. We pressed on and rode deeper into the scrub, finally seeing a large concrete monolith. The bomb had been placed on a steel scaffold 30 metres above the ground and detonated right at this spot, with the explosion monitored back at the village.

It was eerie to stand at the site of an atomic explosion, imagining the destruction that had taken place. We saw twisted metal and trinitite, which is melted particles of sand that are still radioactive. Note to self—don't touch anything! We took a few pictures and didn't hang around too long, but it was amazing to experience something of Australia's hidden history.

About 40 kilometres east of Emu Field, we came across our first fellow traveller for a couple of days. John was heading to Laverton in a beat up old 80 series LandCruiser. He was out exploring like us, with just his dog for company—a real bushy.

We had a chat and said we were headed for Coober Pedy, which was still about 230 kilometres away. John scoffed and said, 'You'll never make that today.' I assured him that our mighty DRs were speedy little ships of the desert, and we'd have no trouble covering that distance. He was amazed, as he was crawling along the rough track very slowly.

Our accommodation for that night was the Mud Hut Motel, in the centre of Coober Pedy, which we made by early afternoon. We'd shipped replacement tyres to the motel to swap over for the next leg. The slabbing on the tar at the beginning of our trip had taken a toll, and our rear tyres were about 50 per cent worn—not ideal for the bigger sand dunes of the Madigan.

We put out a call on social media asking if anyone in town could help us change a couple of tyres. What we actually wanted was someone to change them for us! After the day's riding we'd had, neither Farmer nor I was keen to bust out our tyre levers that afternoon. Much to my amazement, we were quickly in contact with Greg Sparrow, a local adventure rider and all-round good bloke. He steered us to his mate's backyard shop, where we met Franz.

Franz had a yard the size of two large house blocks, full of every type of old Holden you could think of. In his shed were more Holden parts and a few old motorbikes—it was like stepping back in time. I started chatting to him about his collection and soon realised he wasn't aware of the goldmine he was sitting on. Or perhaps he just didn't care and was happy collecting! Franz quickly sorted us out and slapped two new rear tyres on our bikes and we were as good as gold.

The next order of business was a feed. Back in town, we got cleaned up and walked across the road to the pub for a beer or three, followed by a big meal. Camp food only tastes good for so long!

We'd been keeping in contact with Kurtis throughout the ride, as he'd been eagerly following us via Farmer's GPS tracker. We'd been exchanging messages and sending him some photos of our travels, although I was aware it must have been hard for him as he'd been so keen to come.

•

The next day was to be a relatively easy run north to Mount Dare. It was a dirt road but I was hoping for at least a graded surface to ease our aches and pains. We had a leisurely start to the day with a coffee at the roadhouse, before checking over our bikes and refuelling. Then we headed back into the desert.

On the way to Mount Dare, we refuelled at one of the best-known spots in the outback, the Pink Roadhouse at Oodnadatta. Named after the colour it's painted, the Pink Roadhouse is an oasis in the desert, providing all the necessities, as well as good coffee and camel burgers. Every time I've been to the Pink Roadhouse it's been full of tourists, all excited to be out in the desert. You see plenty of big four-wheel drives and off-road caravans, as well as a few motorcyclists like us coming for the adventure of a lifetime.

We topped up our tanks and kept heading north, deeper into desert country. One of the highlights for Farmer was to see the Dalhousie Springs along the way. This is a dam-size body of water from the Great Artesian Basin that is naturally heated underground. It sits on the western edge of the Simpson Desert and travellers flock there. The warm water is high in mineral content and contains little fish that nibble at any exposed skin. Skinny dipping is not recommended! Anyway, we didn't get in for a swim and continued on to Mount Dare, arriving in the early afternoon.

Our plan was to have a rest day at Mount Dare to ensure our bikes were ready to cross the Simpson Desert. It's so remote that you have to ensure all your gear is in good working order before setting off, as there's no prospect of assistance out there for more than 750 kilometres. There's nothing much to do at Mount Dare except eat, drink and socialise with other travellers, and it was while doing this that we met Sean.

Sean told us he was an Irishman living in Melbourne, but he'd had a 'calling' to go back to Ireland. Most people would jump on a plane, but not Sean. His calling, as he told his then girlfriend, involved riding a bicycle from Melbourne all the way around the world, ending in Ireland. Now, I understand the basics of geography, but I'm still not sure that stopping in Mount Dare represented the most direct route! Anyway, Sean was having a great time, camping along the way and relying on handouts from four-wheel drivers. His bike was packed, with things hanging off it all over the place.

Sean was in no rush chatting away as we filled up his water bottles with spare water we'd just bought. What is it with Europeans and bicycle riding in remote Australia? I seem to come across at least one of them every time I venture into the outback.

We spent the next day at Mount Dare filling our water bottles, checking over our bikes and meeting other travellers, ever keen for tips and intel on the track conditions and any hazards that we might encounter. After cleaning up, we headed down to the bar and grabbed a beer, then sat on the verandah to watch the comings and goings in this remote outpost. Over a few hours we sank some beers and chatted away. The good thing about Mount Dare was that there was no mobile phone coverage, so everyone was happy to strike up a conversation to pass the time. That feeling of isolation and disconnection from the outside world was great.

We ate at the pub, knowing it would be our last decent meal for a few days, then turned in quite early. We needed to be well rested for the hard sand riding and dunes that the next day would bring. Just as I was drifting off to sleep, I heard the familiar *bop-bop-bop* of a thumper that sounded suspiciously like a DR650 …

3

And Then There Were Three

Riding my Suzuki TC125 at my hometown of Bribbaree, New South Wales—in all the best protective gear the 80s had to offer! *Richard Barnes*

Leading the way in a Pony Express event at Kowen Forest, Canberra, circa late 1990s.

My first crossing of the Gunbarrel Highway in 2018. A mulga stick pierced the rear tyre of my KTM 990 Adventure S forcing me to repair it in the hot sun of the Gibson Desert.

My previous desert ride in 2022. We stopped at the ghost town of Rawlinna.

The donkey shower at Ilkurlka, a luxury after nights in the bush.

On the 2022 desert ride with Farmer on the Anne Beadell Highway.
Anthony Nicholls

Mamungari Conservation Park, Anne Beadell Highway, 2022. *Anthony Nicholls*

Totem 1 blast site, Emu Field, Great Victoria Desert, 2022. *Anthony Nicholls*

Coober Pedy—there's always an audience at Franz's place. He slapped two new rear tyres on our bikes and we were as good as gold. *Anthony Nicholls*

Three amigos: Kurtis, Farmer and me on our mighty DRs. *Unknown*

Now we're having fun! The Madigan Line in the Simpson Desert boasts great dunes. *Kurtis*

Our second night on the Madigan Line.

2022: just crossed the Madigan Line and contemplating a 2023 Guinness World Record challenge! *Anthony Nicholls*

On top of 'Big Red', the biggest sand dune in the Simpson Desert, a behemoth at nearly 40 metres tall. *Unknown*

Preparing to break a Guinness World Record. My food for the journey was divided into individual daily ration packs. Each pack had to have enough calories to replace what I would be burning that day, and to provide me with the energy I'd need to keep going.

Everything else I carried: I calculated weights for fuel, water and supplies, which when fully loaded would be about 60 kilograms. The key to carrying supplies on the bike is to divide them into smaller quantities and store them in separate areas. That way, if you fall, you don't lose everything all at once.

I WAS WOKEN BY A LOUD BANGING ON OUR DONGA'S FRONT DOOR. Farmer and I sat up in our beds and saw a silhouette against the dark night sky as the door opened. Then we heard a voice: 'What are you old bastards doing in bed at this time?'

It was Kurtis!

The response was just as flattering!

We jumped out of bed, and Kurtis told us how he'd got a short leave pass from home. He had worked out that he could cross the Madigan Line with us if he could get there and back from his home in Victoria in just four days, two days up and two days back. Farmer and I were impressed by his commitment and endurance, as that meant a journey of nearly 2000 kilometres just to meet up with us. To ride that in two days and then tackle the Madigan Line the next day was hardcore.

We got dressed and headed back to the pub so we could continue the conversation over a few more beers. Our best-laid plans of an early night went out the window.

The Madigan Line is in the northern section of the Simpson Desert, and crosses in an east–west direction, just like the French Line below it. It was named after Cecil Madigan, who, leading a party of nine men, made the crossing by camel in 1939. That crossing, about 750 kilometres long, is some 250 kilometres longer than the more popular French Line, and still crosses over sand dunes every kilometre or so. The track is punctuated by about 24 marker posts, where the Madigan team camped overnight. They're replica markers today but you can still recreate Madigan's trek. Because the Madigan Line was longer and more remote than the French Line, we'd need more fuel and water—and that meant very heavy bikes.

The next morning we were keen to get cracking on the next leg of our adventure. We had a cup of coffee—our last decent one for a while—and took a couple of photos before hitting the track.

The Binns Track, which was to be our companion all the way to the start of the Madigan Line, was in bad shape. It was full of deep bulldust holes everywhere. Bulldust is like brown talcum powder: it's a superfine dust that can make the ground appear smooth when actually it hides rocks, ruts and all other nasties underneath, all of which can throw you off your bike as easily as a wild bull. Not only is it dangerous to ride, but it gets into everything that isn't sealed, so your luggage gets coated in it. A bike's air filter can get clogged with the fine particles if you ride in it for too long, or if you follow someone's dust too closely. So we spread out and took it slow and steady, navigating our way through on our heavily laden bikes.

Our first stop for the morning was at Old Andado Station, which was like a time capsule from the 1950s. Back in the day, Andado, which is some 300 kilometres from Alice Springs, was a cattle station of over 10,000 square kilometres—about the size of Lebanon. Molly Clark and her husband, Malcolm 'Mac' Clark, moved there around 1955, when the opportunity came up for them to manage and eventually own the property. Molly was in her early thirties and had three young sons when she arrived there. Life there was hard, with none of the modern conveniences and technology we take for granted now, but the Clarks were tough and self-sufficient.

When we arrived, we were met by the current station caretakers, Jen and her husband, who kindly showed us around. Walking through the old homestead, I could appreciate the hardships the Clarks must have endured. Everything was just like it had been 50 or more years earlier—there were no displays or roped-off areas. I saw the old-fashioned valve radio that was the station's primary form of communications with the outside world. It remained untouched, just as it was back in the day, absolutely amazing.

It was there that we met Matt on his KTM 690. He was also intending to cross the Madigan, but solo a couple of days later. We had a look at his bike, which had a few trick bits here and there, but noticeably was missing a muffler. Matt said he'd lost it on the corrugations during the previous day's riding. He was going to knock up a makeshift muffler and glue it to the rear tailpipe before hitting the trail. We were sceptical about this idea but wished him luck and said we hoped to catch up with him somewhere down the road. I was quietly hoping he'd change his mind, as I didn't want to read about a fellow rider getting into trouble out here.

As we moved on from Old Andado Station, the track gradually became sandier. It really opened right up until we reached the Mac Clark Conservation Reserve, which contains a very rare tree, the *Acacia peuce* or Birdsville wattle. Apparently, it only grew in three nearby regional areas and was a threatened species. After a quick pause we moved past the reserve, keen to get onto the Madigan Line. I couldn't wait to see the first marker post.

The road eventually gave way to a sandy undulating twin track, which made my DR's limited suspension work hard: we were bouncing along like we were on pogo sticks, in and out of the bumpy wheel ruts. Even though I'd had some suspension work done, I quickly realised my suspension was too soft for the load I was carrying, and it was slowing me down a lot. The forks and shock were compressing so much that they only had a couple of inches of travel left through the undulations, which was being transmitted straight up to the handlebars. If I hit any of the undulations too fast, the bike's front wheel would deflect and spear me off the side of the track. For kilometre after kilometre I struggled with this, cursing at how hard the going had become so early on. This wasn't what I'd signed up for.

Finally we reached the first of the sand dunes. I'd had only limited sand dune experience before, and I was nervous and excited to tackle them. Sand riding is tough, and I think my enthusiasm was masking just how tired I was becoming.

We planned to break up the 750 kilometres into a four-day, three-night ride, so we'd taken the pace quite easy. That gave us regular opportunities to stop and have a look around, and I got to practise my dune riding for a few hours. Up and down we went all afternoon, and I slowly realised that the faster you go, the easier it is. Riding faster makes the bike sit on top of the sand, which makes it more stable. But getting a heavy bike up to speed makes for an interesting time. Oh well! I had plenty more dunes to practise on.

In the late afternoon the sun started fading and we had to find a campsite. Luckily enough, just over the crest was a nice clearing. Kurtis led the way and we pulled in and began to set up camp. It was only then that I realised Kurtis had managed to set us up in the Simpson Desert's largest cathead bindi farm—they were enormous, and sticking into everything. *Tribulus terrestris*, or catheads as they are colloquially known, are nasty. They are the size of a thumbtack, with several woody spikes that will penetrate the soles of your feet, your thongs and your airbed. Stepping on one will have you crying out in pain. We could barely move without treading on them or having them stick into our tyres. But we were all too tired to move on, so we cleared the area as best we could.

It was great having new company around the campfire, and soon we were all telling stories and eagerly anticipating what the Madigan Line had in store for us. I'd be lying if I said I wasn't a bit concerned that night about my sand-riding skills. The mystique of the Madigan, combined with my heavy bike, had me wondering if I'd bitten off more than I could chew.

Later in the evening I slipped into my tent and continued reading my book. Benji had decided on a change in lifestyle, so had purchased a dirt bike and moved up to northern Australia, where he had started riding around the Top End. Some interesting stories about riding started twigging my interest. I love reading about other people's experiences in the outback, especially on a dirt bike.

•

The next morning we were chomping at the bit to get going on the dunes again, but I remained concerned about just how heavy my bike was. Had I packed too much? Would I be able to ride the dunes all day? Did I have the stamina? Such worries plagued me as we headed out.

On the straight approaches to the dunes, I was okay: my steering damper was wound up tight and I gunned it as much as I dared. This gave me confidence to go faster and start enjoying the ride a bit more. Around the middle of the morning, Farmer was riding ahead of me and Kurtis behind. I was bouncing along, trying to keep moving in a straight line, when I saw in the distance a massive red sand dune with a small speck on the top. As I approached, I saw that speck was Farmer, who was poised there with his camera. I knew something was up.

As I got closer, I could see that the sand was really deep and soft, with wheel tracks going in all directions. At the base of the dune there was also a sharp left-hand turn, which prevented you from gaining enough speed to get over the top. But I couldn't stop to consider what line to take—I had to keep moving to gain as much speed as I could.

I managed to get up to about 40 kph in second gear and hit the dune as hard as I could. I ended up getting bounced sideways on the approach, causing me to lose momentum. I shifted down into first gear, straddled my bike and dog-paddled all the way up. I revved the crap out of the little DR right up to the top while pushing as hard as I could with my legs. I couldn't stop or I wouldn't make it. *Just keep going!* I screamed to myself. It wasn't pretty but I made it.

All the while, Farmer stood silently with his camera focused on the action. What are friends for! My chest was heaving as I tried to suck in all the available air around me on top of that dune.

I'd barely got my breath back when I heard the roar of Kurtis approaching at fast pace and saw him bouncing all over the track. He shot up the face next to me, jumping about two feet in the air, before landing crossed up sideways and disappearing down the other side. God knows how he stayed on, but it made for a great video!

We made good progress that day, with my sand-riding skills improving over each dune. So were Farmer's. I didn't know it but he'd been riding the whole time without a steering damper, and he was starting to develop forearms like Popeye from hanging on.

We didn't see another person all that day. The Madigan is not a well-travelled route, and the solitude was great—just three mates and their bikes. We had it all to ourselves.

One of the things about camping in the desert is the night sky. As we set up camp that night, the sky was brilliant, with satellites zooming across the field. It was a cold night, so we made sure our campfire was roaring as we sat around eating our camp meals and bragging about who had done it easiest in the sand that day.

I read a bit more of my book that night. Benji was also getting into a bit of sand riding, on Fraser Island on his little Yamaha WR250. This was something I could relate to as I'd been to Fraser Island before, albeit in a four-wheel drive. I was enjoying the story much more now.

Our last day on the Madigan Line would see us push through to Adria Downs Station. Adria Downs is an 8750-square-kilometre cattle station on the edge of the Simpson Desert where the Madigan Line passes through. We'd obtained permission from the station to travel through this section of it. We still hadn't heard from our friend at Old Andado Station on his mufflerless KTM 690, so we figured he'd shown some caution and waited until he could get it repaired properly.

The dunes continued, and so did the camp markers. By then I'd used up a lot of the fuel I was carrying on the back of the bike, and drunk a fair bit of water, so the bike was feeling a little better. I wasn't struggling so much under its weight and was generally having an easier time. After the previous days of sand dune riding I felt I was tackling them much better, hitting them in third gear and cresting easily.

It was at around camp 15 that we would head south on the Hay River Track, which would be much easier as we would be running parallel to the dunes for a while, and not going over them. The ground in between the dunes was still sandy but had a hard base underneath.

We passed a couple of four-wheel drives travelling in the other direction and stopped for the obligatory chat and discussion about the track conditions. As we got going again, Farmer, Kurtis and I reminded each other to keep an eye out when cresting dunes as there appeared to be more traffic heading in our direction. I had fitted up UHF radio communications to my helmet but it was a bit hit and miss, and not all drivers were announcing their locations.

We eventually made it across the Hay River Track and onto some station tracks on Adria Downs. It was a lot of fun riding parallel to the dunes for a bit—lighter bikes, speeds a bit faster, life was good. We pulled up every hour or so to have a rest, and it was now that I realised Farmer was not a happy camper. His forearms had taken an absolute pounding. He was buggered and wanted to stop—right now! It took a bit of coaxing to get him to ride on a little further, to a more suitable campsite off the beaten track for the night.

We had conquered the Madigan! Wow, what a feeling. This was my first Simpson Desert crossing, and doing it on the Madigan Line was amazing. I was so pleased with myself for completing it, and felt real satisfaction wash over me that night. I went to bed feeling elated and opened my book, reading with more and more vigour as Benji began looking for a new challenge in his life and the story of his Guinness World Record attempt emerged. This really caught my interest.

•

The next day we got moving towards Birdsville. It was fairly easy going until the left turn onto the QAA Line, where we encountered the dunes of death. Wow! I'd thought the dunes on the Madigan Line were big, but they were nothing compared to those between Eyre Creek and Birdsville. They culminated in the form of 'Big Red', the biggest of them all, a behemoth at nearly 40 metres tall. This was the last challenge to get us out of the desert.

We all lined up at the bottom. I went first, snicked up to third gear, pinned it and hung on. I made it and was now on top of the world, mission completed. Next came Kurtis. He must have been in fourth gear, as he jumped about four feet in the air at the crest. Finally came Farmer, but without a steering damper he wasn't able to hit it as hard. He was going great and Kurtis and I were yelling encouragement, but it wasn't to be, with his bike bogging down about ten metres from the crest. With a bit of help, he also made it to the top. The three amigos had crossed the Simpson—what a feeling!

I decided that I liked this desert riding, and my mind briefly wandered back to the ten deserts challenge I'd been reading about.

We took the obligatory photos at the top and enjoyed the easy ride into Birdsville. The caravan park was our oasis in the desert for a couple of nights. Never was a hot shower more welcome.

That night, we all enjoyed a few too many beers and a steak at the Birdsville Hotel, meeting many more travellers and swapping stories of our adventures. That's another great thing about being out there: no one's a local, and everyone has a story to tell. It's a combination that makes for great conversation and a fun night.

The next morning Kurtis was off, as he had to get home. The night before, he'd met a bloke riding a Husqvarna TR 650 who was travelling in the same direction, so they agreed to ride together for part of the day. We all met up at the bakery for breakfast before saying our goodbyes. Farmer and I planned to spend an extra day in town, resting and doing bike maintenance.

I found some time during the day to finish off my book. Benji had planned a ride through all ten Australian deserts and completed it, earning himself a Guinness World Record as the first person to do so. I couldn't believe what I was reading—this was an ordinary bloke just like me, but he'd achieved a truly extraordinary feat. I felt an excitement building within me. I'd already ridden eight of the ten deserts over the years, and now I'd just completed the Madigan Line. *I could do that*, I said to myself.

Right at that moment, my destiny was set. This would be my next challenge. I knew already that I wouldn't stop thinking about it until it was done.

Our journey was at an end—but it had been so much more than a journey. Every time I travelled into the outback, I felt a strong connection with the bush: it relaxed me and helped me clear my head. This time, it had filled my mind with plans that would consume me for the year ahead.

4

Gearing Up

I arrived home on 17 July 2022 and hadn't been there five minutes before I was telling my wife, Stace, about my new plans. I saw a look in her eyes that said: *You've just come back!*

We sat down to talk it over and I convinced her I was serious: I was going to attempt to break a Guinness World Record. It would be a huge undertaking and I didn't know how or where to start. I'd found it easy to plan recreational rides, but breaking a world record was next level. I mulled the idea over for a week or two, going over my previous ride plans and maps, and came up with a rough idea of what I needed to do. Already I knew that, if I was going to pull this off, I had a lot to learn.

One of the first conditions I imposed on my challenge was that I would only ride during daylight hours. This was a rule I had adhered to all my riding life, and for good reason. Riding a motorcycle in the bush at night is very dangerous, due to the amount of wildlife you can run into. There are kangaroos, emus, camels, cattle and more kangaroos, just to name a few, and a collision with any of them can be life-threatening. I would be comfortable riding from dawn to dusk and no longer. With those parameters in mind, I got cracking.

First I had to find out exactly where the ten Australian deserts were! I'd never even considered how many deserts there were in the country. I'd crossed some on previous rides, but I had to find out where they all were to give me a clearer idea of the route I'd need to design. I didn't know if there were roads or tracks passing through all of them. But I knew that Guinness World Records doesn't just hand out world records casually, so I had to get serious.

In my research I discovered that Australia actually has more than ten deserts by name, but there are only ten deserts recognised geographically. These were the ones I had to cross.

The ten deserts of Australia, listed by size, are:

1. The Great Victoria Desert: 348,750 square kilometres
2. The Great Sandy Desert: 267,250 square kilometres
3. The Tanami Desert: 184,500 square kilometres
4. The Simpson Desert: 176,500 square kilometres
5. The Gibson Desert: 156,000 square kilometres
6. The Little Sandy Desert: 111,500 square kilometres
7. The Strzelecki Desert: 80,250 square kilometres
8. The Sturt Stony Desert: 29,750 square kilometres
9. The Tirari Desert: 15,250 square kilometres
10. The Pedirka Desert: 1250 square kilometres

They're spread out centrally across the continent, with the largest portion occupying the Western Australian landmass, about as far away from my home in Canberra as I could get. This was going to be an epic ride. There were huge variances in size, and I would have to make sure my route traversed through all of them to the satisfaction of Guinness World Records.

I would spend the next year reading and researching everything I could about each of these desert areas: their geographical boundaries, the climate during the winter months, whether any water was available in each of them, whether there were roads that crossed them, and the type of terrain I would encounter. And it wasn't only the deserts I needed to know about, it was also the availability of fuel supplies in the deserts, whether that be from cattle stations, Aboriginal communities or roadhouses. Fortunately, I had a thirst for information; I knew I had to prepare myself and my bike properly for such a rugged adventure.

The current record set by Benji Brundin was 29 days, 19 hours and 38 minutes and my initial plans were for a 20-day assault. I thought this was quite conservative, as I wouldn't be riding at night or travelling crazy distances each day. I based my estimates on distances I had already travelled on previous trips under similar conditions. As I learned more about the deserts I hadn't ridden, I could fine-tune them further. Within this estimated timeframe, there was room for me to push harder if I could but I didn't want to put too much pressure on myself.

I eventually settled on a plan with my route commencing at Marree in South Australia and heading to Birdsville in Queensland, where I would cross the Tirari, Strzelecki and Sturt Stony deserts. After that I would briefly enter the Northern Territory, before re-entering South Australia making for Coober Pedy, crossing the Simpson and Pedirka Deserts in the process. Travelling on I would continue westward into Western Australia to cross the Great Victoria Desert, then taking a more northerly direction to enter and then cross the Gibson Desert before heading westward again for the township of Wiluna. After Wiluna I would ride the entire Canning Stock Route, crossing the Little Sandy and Great Sandy deserts, before turning right towards the Northern Territory again and across the Tanami Desert. My route would finish at the township of Yuendumu.

There were two deserts I had not yet crossed on previous rides, they were the Little Sandy and Great Sandy deserts along the Canning Stock Route. These were the tough ones, and the ones I was most concerned about. The others I was looking forward to riding again, albeit all at once, but at least I had some prior knowledge which eased my mind.

I was quite happy with this route; it covered all the deserts and I calculated the distance to be somewhere between 5000 and 6000 kilometres dependent upon detours and/or track closures. Using my knowledge from prior desert rides I was able to plan out daily distances that I thought were achievable, which would give me my overall timeframe. This was something I would play around with, forecasting different durations to complete the trip.

•

Along with my logistical planning, I turned my mind to how I would prepare myself physically for the journey. I was a 55-year-old guy of average fitness, and I wanted to give myself the best chance I could of completing the ride. I've always been decently 'bike fit', and this had seen me through my previous desert trips in good shape, but this ride would be different. This wasn't a holiday—it was a non-stop marathon across the country. It would involve day after day of hard physical activity for hours on end, and my bike fitness would only get me so far.

To increase my physical fitness, I turned to two of my other favourite pastimes: mountain bike riding and hiking. These would help increase my endurance and improve my cardiovascular fitness. I wanted to increase my stamina so I could better handle the hard riding and long days.

I hadn't ridden my mountain bike for some time, so I dusted it off and got it ready for regular use. Canberra has a great network of bike paths and trails, and I started clocking up the kilometres. I forced myself to ride that bike every afternoon, in the heat, the cold, the wind or the rain. I was driven to succeed and this was an important aspect that would help me do that. My regular ride was a lap around Lake Burley Griffin, the central lake and major feature of Canberra. This is about 26 kilometres, and I aimed to cover that distance in an hour or less. The route was hilly and picturesque, and I'd put on my headphones and zone out, dreaming of the desert while pedalling like a lunatic for an hour.

A 26-kilometre ride might not sound like much to a passionate cyclist, but I got my heart rate up and kept it there while pushing myself harder each time. Eventually the hills got flatter and my times became quicker. I could see the improvements in my fitness levels, and my heart wasn't racing quite as hard as when I'd started. I really enjoyed my time on the bike on Canberra's sunny days, but on the many cold and miserable days I had to dig deep.

Being near the Snowy Mountains and not far from the coast, Canberra has some of the best hiking trails in Australia. As well as increasing my fitness, my regular treks gave me a chance to trial some new gear I'd bought for my ride, including a new CamelBak Military Spec hydration backpack. I wanted to carry a slightly larger backpack than I had for previous rides so I could pack in my day rations, a first-aid kit and plenty of water.

I also wanted to test out a new Garmin inReach satellite tracker and messenger. This little device would enable me to summon the rescue gods in the event of an emergency anywhere in the world, with or without a mobile phone signal. It also sent and received SMS messages via satellite, which was great for keeping in touch with family and friends.

Stace is a keen hiker, though mainly in the winter months as she is scared of snakes. One weekend we went for a trip to Sussex Inlet, on the New South Wales south coast. I'd planned a nice 15-kilometre hike through bushland, coastal headland and beach. It would be the perfect place to trial my new backpack and Garmin. The weather was reasonably warm, and Stace was being brave venturing into the bush during the summertime. I filled my three-litre hydration bladder, packed all the snacks I would for a day ride, and enclosed my full first-aid kit as well. I wanted the pack to be as close to the exact weight as it would be on the ride.

Off we went, meandering through the coastal bushland, seeing wallabies hopping around and white cockatoos screeching. Eventually we came to the most magnificent flat, sandy beach. We took our shoes off and walked in the cool water for the last few kilometres of the hike. It was bliss. I was very pleased with how comfy the backpack was, and the little Garmin attached to the shoulder strap offered safety and security.

Over the next twelve months, I rode and hiked, and incorporated a lot of stretching and some weight training too. If I fell off my heavy bike, I needed to be able to pick it up again. It was sometimes hard to stay motivated, but when I felt like wimping out I visualised holding that Guinness World Record certificate, and that always got me moving again. The last thing I wanted was for my body to let me down.

•

By now I'd identified all the tracks I needed to take through Australia's ten deserts, and I started working on daily distances and resupply points. A lot of the tracks passed through either Indigenous lands or Defence prohibited areas, both of which required permits. There were a number of different Aboriginal land councils I had to contact, and each used a different form and required different information, including my proposed dates. Forecasting these dates nearly twelve months in advance was quite difficult, for a number of reasons.

Firstly, the Defence land I had to travel through was the Woomera Prohibited Zone, which closes at certain times each year. But in this zone was the road I chose to cross the Great Victoria Desert, the Anne Beadell Highway, which I had to use. So I had to align all the dates on my permits so I could avoid the Defence closures. I also had to factor in the desert riding season, when the temperatures were favourable. All this required a huge amount of administrative work.

In the end, I was left with a fairly narrow window of opportunity in which to undertake my Guinness World Record attempt. If that had been the only consideration, it would have been easy enough to keep my dates set—but in the Top End there's an isolated little place called Burketown that had other ideas.

Burketown is named after the famous Australian explorer Robert O'Hara Burke, who, along with his travelling companion, William John Wills, was the first to cross the Australian continent from south to north. They travelled all the way from Melbourne to the Gulf of Carpentaria, where Burketown sits.

In March 2023, Burketown received days of torrential rainfall, causing massive flooding. All that floodwater was heading south, into the northern Queensland channel country and eventually into Lake Eyre, in Central Australia. These waters would reach the southern desert region in the middle of the desert riding season, right when I wanted to leave, and they would cut across my planned route. Little did I know how much of a headache that would cause me.

•

Because of my previous desert trips, I had a fair idea of what equipment and food I wanted to take. My food was to be prepared in individual daily ration packs. Each pack had to have enough calories to replace what I would be burning that day, and to provide me with the energy I'd need to keep going. I varied the contents of each ration pack for interest's sake, but here's what a typical day's food looked like:

- Breakfast: 1 porridge sachet, 1 coffee sachet
- Day snacks: 1 bag of sugar lollies and 1 bag trail mix (nuts and dried fruit)
- Lunch: 1 tuna sachet
- Day snacks: 1 Muesli bar
- Dinner: 1 dehydrated camp meal, 1 coffee sachet

All the food items were contained within sturdy cliplock bags which could be squashed down flat. This reduced their volume and made them easy to pack into my soft saddlebags.

As I planned to be on the road for twenty days, I couldn't carry all my ration packs at once, so I had to plan some resupply points. This was difficult, as there were limited towns on the route, and making sure my gear got to where I needed it—and stayed there—was a challenge. I ended up sending two resupply packages to the post offices in the towns nearest to where I would be passing. This had to be timed perfectly: send them too early and they might sit there uncollected for too long and be sent back. I made a few calls to the post offices concerned to make sure they had been received and would be there on my arrival. Details like this couldn't be overlooked. Without my two resupply points, the ride would have been impossible.

Next I turned my mind to my water requirements. Some of the places I would be going might not have water available for up to four to five days if all went to plan, longer if it didn't. Obviously, water was crucial to surviving in the desert, but it's also a very heavy commodity, so it was a fine balance. I had a rough idea of how much I used each day from my previous trips, but I wanted some extra capacity in case of emergencies. Thinking about the vast stretches of nothingness in the western deserts made me very conservative in my planning.

The key to carrying supplies on the bike is to divide them into smaller quantities and store them in separate areas. That way, if you fall, you don't lose everything all at once. I already had a set of very hardy, Australian-made canvas saddlebags, which had pockets for water bottles at the front and rear on each side. I filled them with four one and a half-litre heavy-duty plastic water bottles, and also packed two water bladders—one of four litres, the other six. Having this capacity meant they didn't all have to be full all the time, but whenever I was about to embark on a long stretch without water, I would fill them all up. Including my CamelBak, I would then have 19 litres. That would have to do as I was conscious of overloading my bike.

The next most important thing was fuel. My bike was fitted with a commercially available 36-litre long-range fuel tank. I took along two 12-litre fuel bladders as well, which I could roll up and store away when I didn't need them. My last reserve would be a pair of two-litre hard fuel bottles, one in each pannier. That gave me a total fuel capacity of 64 litres. I didn't think I would ever need that much, but of course it was better to be safe than sorry. My bike would consume around six litres per 100 kilometres, giving me a theoretical range of just over 1000 kilometres. I was comfortable with that.

My living quarters consisted of a lightweight one-man hiking tent which weighed under two kilograms. I bought a sleeping pad that had a high insulation rating and was slightly on the larger side. I indulged a little here, as I knew from experience that a good night's sleep was vital to keep me going. I topped this off with a high-quality down sleeping bag with a hood to ensure I stayed toasty warm on the coldest desert nights.

The last of my supplies were to be the tools and spares that I thought I might need along the way. As these would be the heaviest and bulkiest items I was carrying, I had to choose carefully. Little things that could cause the trip to come to a stop were foremost in my mind. I carried spare chain links, a clutch lever and cable, along with an assortment of cable ties, tape, wire, electrical fittings, some liquid steel and plastic sealants. I also had a small but comprehensive tool kit that would allow me to work on every part of the bike if needed. I had developed this kit over years of riding—and breakdowns!

As with my food, water and fuel, I tried to spread the weight of my spares all over the bike. Little tricks like cable-tying the spare lever behind the headlight and routing spare cable along the originals for ease of fitment would make life easier in the event of a breakdown. The tool kit would ride in the bottom of my saddlebags to keep the weight down low and towards the front. This would help centre the additional mass I would be carrying.

•

From my last trip, I knew I had to make a few adjustments to my Suzuki DR650 before I set off on the Guinness World Record attempt. I had a fairly solid set-up before, but I would be carrying a heavier load. I weighed up everything I was taking and calculated weights for fuel, water and supplies, which when fully loaded would be about 60 kilograms. This would be the equivalent of taking a pillion along for the ride. This worried me, as I was concerned about the bike's ability to carry the weight at speed over rough terrain without breaking something.

The subframe on the DR is fairly robust around the seat area, but the steel tubing thins out considerably the further towards the rear you go, so I had to ensure the bulk of the weight was carried across the seat. That was why my soft pannier bags were so good, as they carried all the weight via two main straps right across the pillion seat, where the bracing was at its strongest. This, I hoped, would be sufficient to avoid any breakages.

To help improve the bike's handling with its load, I fitted heavier springs and custom valving to the front and rear suspension. The DR's suspension is a very old design and quite limited in its ability to cope with rough terrain and heavy loads. These adjustments would help the bike ride higher and navigate through the deep sand better. They would also help with the endless corrugations I expected to encounter. I used high-quality suspension fluids, as the constant pounding the suspension was about to take needed the best to prevent it from breaking down. There wasn't much else I did to the bike, as I had bought it for its old-school simplicity. The DRs are renowned worldwide for their reliability, so my mantra was to leave as much of it stock-standard as I could.

Meanwhile, I was keeping an eye on the weather. Early 2023 had been unseasonably wet, with La Niña in full force. The deserts were in bloom and some areas were inaccessible due to groundwater. This, as well as the floods moving south from Burketown, had made my route impassable. I wouldn't be able to start the Guinness World Record attempt in the window I'd planned.

My mind was so full of planning information that at times it felt like it was spinning faster than my bike wheels as I tried to stay on top of all the details, and now Mother Nature was throwing this in as well! I had managed everything in my control, but it was what was out of my control that bugged me. My frustrations were building, and more than once I felt like calling the whole thing off, only for Stace to keep me focused.

•

Another task I had was to obtain pre-approval from Guinness World Records before I set off. During the planning for this Guinness World Record attempt, I had to submit a lot of information, including evidence that the bike I was using was street legal, and all the accessories and modifications were commercially available, it's part of the rules. Along with these details I also had to plan and submit my proposed route for the attempt. It is a painstakingly detailed process.

Given the route details including the finish line of the original record were a little scant and not well defined in my mind, and given the fact that Guinness World Records will not reveal them either, required me to design and submit a route of my own making. One of my considerations was ensuring I could obtain crucial evidence at the start and finish lines of the ride as the rules required two witnesses at each location. It appeared that the existing record finished somewhere along the Tanami Road which didn't sit well with me. Being a details-oriented guy, it worried me trying to prove that I had finished in the middle of nowhere with no one around. To comply with the rules, I set my start and finish line in a town to ensure there were people around to be witnesses. I thought this would make my ride longer than the original route but at least I would have peace of mind knowing that it would be well documented. The last thing I wanted to do was get to the finish line only to not have the evidence to prove it!

I remember being on edge from the time I submitted my pre-approval request to Guinness World Records, waiting for the familiar *ding* of an email alert on my phone. Every time one arrived, I instantly checked my emails, until I finally got the message I was waiting for. It came from Lewis, my Guinness World Records application manager, and he informed me that my record attempt had been approved. I jumped up and down with excitement—I had the green light! This positive news offered welcome respite after the weeks of worry I'd had about the flooding.

So I had my permits and my pre-approval from Guinness World Records; now all I needed was the right weather.

I had found a good source of information in the form of the local police at the little outback towns near my route. They all got to know my name, as I rang them often and bugged them for information about road conditions and closures. Their invaluable local knowledge allowed me to set a date for the start of my ride.

Shortly after my Guinness World Records approval came through, the Birdsville police told me the flooding had hit the Simpson Desert, cutting the main crossing on Eyre Creek. The desert was now impassable and the crossing was to be assessed during the next two- to six-week period. My heart sank—I would have to postpone again! Would I even be able to make the attempt this year? When would the route be open? When would the water subside? My mind was racing with questions.

I was disappointed and frustrated at the same time. Stace could sense my mood and was a constant source of positive energy for me during these down times, reassuring me that things would work out. I just couldn't see it then.

The delay meant I had to get all my permits reissued with new dates, which I had to calculate based on when I thought the water level in Eyre Creek would be low enough to cross. It was not an exact science: even with all my research, there were no reliable estimates available. It was all guesswork. I factored in the crossing's opening being delayed by a further two weeks after its initial reopening date to give me some margin of error. This proved a wise decision, as the initial reopening was indeed delayed by a fortnight.

The elation I felt when I received the news in July that Eyre Creek was open was like a shot of adrenaline. It was on—I was going! I had been told the water had receded enough to allow four-wheel drives and motorbikes through, but I had no information that motorbikes were capable to cross with the current water level due to their shallower fording ability compared to that of a four-wheel drive vehicle. Would I be the first? Or would the water still be too deep? My anxiety as I waited to find out tied my stomach in knots for days.

5

No Turning Back

20 July

My starting point was at Marree, in South Australia, nearly 2000 kilometres from home, so I wanted to get on the road nice and early. The car was loaded with all my gear, checked, double-checked and triple-checked as well. I hooked up the bike trailer with my trusty DR650 strapped down tightly and had one last look over it. It was then hugs from Stace, who wished me luck and a safe trip. The emotion of the moment hit me: the next time I'd see her, I was hoping to have set a new Guinness World Record.

The drive to Marree was to take me three days, with stopovers in Balranald, in New South Wales, and Peterborough, in South Australia. The first day was fairly uneventful, the only event of note coming when I stopped to help a lady with a flat tyre on the side of the highway. As I drove, I encouraged myself to relax, knowing what lay ahead. I made a few calls to friends while I was driving to calm my nerves, before overnighting at a local pub.

The next day my mind started whirring again, and I went over the last conversation I'd had with the Birdsville copper about Eyre Creek. He'd told me that four-wheel drives were crossing and that I should be able to push my bike through. But what did that actually mean? Four-wheel drives have a higher clearance than motorbikes, and he wasn't able to tell me with any certainty how deep the water was. Was there a current? What was the base of the creek like? Would I be able to get across?

During breaks on the way up to Marree, I scoured social media and websites for reports from people who had crossed Eyre Creek. They were few and far between as it had only just opened, which added to my concern. If I couldn't get across Eyre Creek, the rest of my Guinness World Record attempt would be for nothing. I was feeling stressed.

The next day was overcast and sprinkling rain as I drove into South Australia. I hoped it would stop by the time I reached the desert country. In Peterborough, I pulled into a local caravan park and got chatting to Neil Walker, who happened to be the owner. He was interested in my bike and asked me what I was up to. When I told him what I was about to attempt in order to break a Guinness World Record, he couldn't believe it. It turned out he was also an adventure rider, and also owned a DR, so he was impressed by what I was trying to do on the humble little Suzuki. We chatted for quite a while and he told me he was also the owner of one of the local pubs. Needless to say, an hour or so later saw me sitting at the bar having a beer. A great time was had that night chatting to the locals. Neil wished me well on my adventures the next day and invited me to drop in on my way back.

Leaving Peterborough, I travelled up through the beautiful Flinders Ranges to Marree, which sits on the edge of the Tirari Desert. For hours the Flinders Ranges were on my right-hand side, the sun contrasting their reddish colours with the green of the scrubby saltbush country. It was a magnificent sight.

It was only about 400 kilometres the next day up to Marree, although with all I had on my mind I forgot to fuel up the car and so I was running on fumes when I crawled into Hawker. After a fill-up there, I arrived in Marree early in the afternoon.

Now my nerves really started to kick in. I'd booked accommodation and a place to leave my vehicle and trailer, so that was all sorted. I drove to the only service station in town and filled up all my fuel tanks: diesel for the car and unleaded for the bike. There was no need to fill up my fuel bladders for the first day's riding as the distance wasn't that great.

Marree hadn't changed much since my last visit a few years before: everything was as I remembered it, right down to the club building of the famous Lake Eyre Yacht Club. The town also sports two enormous, faded red diesel locomotives. Remnants of the old Ghan railway from years gone by, they are the centrepiece of the township. All in all, I felt quite at home here.

Later that afternoon, once I had got settled in my cabin, I walked back over to the service station, which doubled as a cafe, and ordered a meal. I got talking to one of the ladies working there and was telling her about why I was in town and what I was about to do. After we'd finished chatting, a bloke sitting in the corner of the cafe called out, 'Hey, mate—have you got a minute?' so I walked over.

He'd overheard the conversation I was having and was interested to talk. He told me he was in town with a group of others for the Heart 2 Heart long-distance charity walk which had started in the centre of Australia heading for Canberra to raise awareness and support for the mental health of first responders. After a minute or so, we realised that—remarkably—we knew each other! Who would have thought that here, in the middle of nowhere, I'd run into Paul, an old colleague? It had been at least ten years since our paths last crossed, and we had a good old laugh about it. We exchanged details and promised to track each other's movements over the coming days.

•

The next day I got up early. I wanted to be up for sunrise so I knew what time I could leave the following day. Once there was sufficient daylight, I made a note of the time—7.30am—this would be my departure time tomorrow morning. This was the last of the planning; soon it would be time for the doing.

When the sun was up, I unloaded my bike from the trailer and had another look over it. Even though I'd done this countless times before, it made me feel good. The DR fired up straightaway, which was comforting, then it settled into a steady idle. This was my last chance to discover any problems with the bike, so I dressed in my riding gear and took it for a short shakedown along some of the dirt tracks out of town. Thankfully there were no issues. I spent the rest of the day going over logistics and supplies, making sure I had everything I needed.

There was a stream of messages from my family and friends later in the day. I felt supported by this tremendous group of people, who were all wishing me luck and encouraging me for the challenge ahead.

6

Nemesis

24 July

THE NIGHT BEFORE I LEFT, I SLEPT REALLY BADLY—TWO OR THREE hours at most. In the silence of the pre-dawn, it was just me and my thoughts. My bed at the Marree caravan park wasn't all that comfortable but it was my mind that had kept me awake. It had been going overtime all night, running through checklists—had I done this, did I bring that, don't forget to do this. So I wasn't well rested when I eventually got out of bed.

Even though I was tired, I felt a strong urge to get moving. I got up and put the kettle on and made a coffee, then got on with my preparations. I methodically packed my bike, strapping things down, working slowly so I didn't miss anything. As I checked things over, I found it hard to believe I was actually getting ready to attempt to break a Guinness World Record. I'd been planning for this moment for a year now, and it had finally arrived.

I had met a group of three guys the night before—Dave, George and Peter—who were on their way to do their first Simpson Desert crossing in their four-wheel drive. They were a great bunch of blokes and happy to chat, and were interested in what I was up to. In the end they'd agreed to see me off and be witnesses to the start of my ten-desert adventure. As I mentioned earlier one of the Guinness World Record requirements was that I had to obtain at least two witness statements from the start, and Dave and George were happy to oblige. They were to complement whatever other witnesses I could obtain to verify my location during my journey.

As the sun started rising over the horizon and the townscape slowly emerged from the darkness, I heard the familiar rustling of bodies in tents starting to wake up. Not long after, Dave and his friends emerged. I boiled the kettle again and had another coffee with them, and we chatted about the day ahead. They seemed just as excited as I was.

Finally I was ready. I put all my bike gear on, started the bike and made sure all my GPS and tracking equipment was working. I took a couple of photos with the guys before jumping on the bike. With a pull of the clutch lever, the little Suzuki was in first gear and I was away. It felt great!

My route today of approximately 600 kilometres would take me north through three deserts, the Tirari, Strzelecki and Sturt Stony deserts, hopefully ending up in the Simpson Desert and across Eyre Creek. It would be a mixture of dirt roads of varying condition, then sand dunes, finally finishing with the flooded crossing at Eyre Creek. I wanted to get to Eyre Creek as fast as possible—I needed to know whether I could cross it—so this was my objective today.

I rode off slowly in the early dawn light, trying to read the surface of the dirt road against the shortening shadows. I set an easy pace to get the bike warmed up, and so I could get used to the load I was carrying. I was grinning from ear to ear in my helmet, all my tiredness washed away. Now it was just me and my bike, the way I liked it, and it would be that way for some time.

It was awesome being out in the desert again. The open plains and barren landscapes are unlike anything you experience in the eastern states. Riding along, you can see the vastness of the plains over the low-lying saltbush scrub. There was not another person to be seen, not even any wildlife, and just my bike engine cutting through the silence.

I had set my bike up with a tall gear ratio for this stage of the trip, which allowed me to ride a bit faster without over-revving the motor. The DR was built with five gears, not six like more modern dirt bikes, so it tended to rev a bit higher if not geared correctly. The track to Birdsville was mostly deep gravel, with some sandy patches scattered in as well. There were enough variations in the road surfaces to keep me paying attention, so I couldn't do much daydreaming.

Even so, this stretch of track brought back memories of a previous trip, back in 2011, when I was returning from Cape York Peninsula on my KTM 990 Adventure S. I had camped at Birdsville the previous night, intending to ride down to Marree and grab a scenic flight over Lake Eyre, which was in flood that year as well. The Birdsville Track had been cut in half by the swollen Cooper Creek. As it's the only direct road joining the two towns, the South Australian government had employed a ferryman to operate a ferry across the flooded Cooper Creek. So for a few months that year outback travellers were treated to a ferry ride in the Tirari Desert. The ferryman ended up living out there for some months, operating the ferry as needed and sleeping in his nearby caravan when not. He was a friendly type and loved a chat—I suppose travellers were his main contacts.

There was one stop along the way to Birdsville this time, a little outback roadhouse called Mungerannie. It was literally an oasis in the desert along the Birdsville Track. One minute you're riding along all alone, and then you pop over a rise in the track and see a small outback roadhouse and petrol pumps. By the time I arrived at the Mungerannie roadhouse, I'd already crossed through the Tirari and part of the Strzelecki deserts, so was making good progress. I pulled in for a stretch and a rest. I didn't really need to fill up with fuel, but there's a golden rule in the Australian outback: never knock back fuel when you can get it. So I duly topped up my tank and pushed on to Birdsville.

Birdsville is a famous outback town in far western Queensland renowned for its annual horse race, music festival and the iconic Birdsville Hotel. As the saying goes, there are no strangers there, just friends you haven't met, and I can attest to the truth of that. I'd spent a few nights enjoying the hospitality there. Birdsville has a population of about 110 people and a few dogs in normal times, but that swells to well over 10,000 when these events are on, bringing in people from all over the country. But as soon as the events are over, it is back to being a quiet little town again.

Birdsville's other major drawcard is its location on the eastern edge of the Simpson Desert, making it the primary supply point for any crossing westward to Mount Dare.

By midafternoon I'd made it into Birdsville, and crossed desert number three the Sturt Stony Desert in good time. This time I filled up the tank and put a few litres in one of my fuel bladders. I'd received instructions that a bypass track around Eyre Creek was open, but I wasn't sure exactly how much extra distance it would add to my route. The crossing to Mount Dare was approximately 500 kilometres of hardcore sand riding, and I'd been told the creek bypass might add an additional 60 kilometres. Things aren't always exact in the outback, so I had to factor in a margin for error. I managed to get some water and snacks into me and fitted a smaller front sprocket to give me more low-down torque for the sand dunes I'd be climbing for the next day or so.

•

The next leg of the trip through the Simpson would start on the QAA Line, heading west from Birdsville, and then take me onto the French Line. This is the most direct route through the Simpson but also the toughest. It has no less than 1000 sand dunes to cross, so isn't for the faint-hearted. The Simpson Desert is the most popular in the country. It receives more tourists during the winter months than all the other deserts combined. It's popular with dirt bike riders, four-wheel drivers, pushbike riders and even walkers, so there can be a lot of traffic out there.

There are two ways to enter the Simpson Desert from the eastern side: over the sand dune known as 'Little Red', or over its bigger brother—'Big Red'. Having tackled Big Red the year before on our Madigan Line trip, I had nothing to prove and everything to lose if I fell or got bogged, so I took the safer option over Little Red. *Ride smart*, I thought to myself.

As soon as I hit the deep sand going up Little Red, though, things got loose. The bike bucked and bounced, and the front wheel veered right and left. I got over the top and down the bottom, then stopped straightaway. I checked my steering damper and only then remembered to set it firmer, to compensate for the effect the sand was having on my front wheel.

I checked everything was tied down securely, turned on my UHF radio so I could communicate with the four-wheel drivers in the dunes, then took off again. I made sure to ride faster this time as my bike was heavy and needed to get on top of the sand to increase its stability. As I've explained, speed can make the bike handle better, but it can also put you into the bull-bar of a four-wheel drive on the crest of a dune, so it's a fine balance.

The first dozen or so sand dunes of the QAA Line are the biggest. Travelling from east to west was harder than coming from the opposite direction due to the shape of the dune faces, which are steeper and more chopped up on their eastern sides. This is because the prevailing wind blows against the face of the dunes, and because of the constant scalloping out of the wheel tracks by the many four-wheel drives spinning their tyres on their way up the face. The only way to combat that on a motorbike is with speed. Trust in your steering damper to keep things straight, and your suspension to soak up the scallops. Mind you, some of the scallops nearly buried my bike, they were that deep.

In these conditions, I was standing on the foot pegs constantly, letting the bike move around under me as I raced up the face of another dune and then cruised down the other side. I called my location often on the UHF radio to alert nearby four-wheel drives of my presence.

About 30 kilometres along the QAA Line, I saw the detour markers for the bypass track. The track now turned due north and ran parallel to the dunes, into much firmer ground which was easier to ride. I knew there was only about 30 kilometres between me and my fate. Would Eyre Creek be crossable by bike? I still didn't know.

The ride down the bypass track was really enjoyable, fast and flowing, and I found a really good rhythm. The sun had moved into the afternoon sky, giving me only a few more hours of daylight, so I was feeling a bit of pressure to get this done. After about half an hour, I rounded a bend in the track and got my first view of Eyre Creek. Shit!

Eyre Creek was in full flood. The water was rushing and in parts looked over 40 metres wide. I just couldn't see how I'd get across and felt my stomach tighten up as I approached. I rode on for another kilometre or so, desperately hoping it would be shallower and narrower.

At the crossing, the creek had narrowed to about 30 metres wide but was still flowing fairly quick. The crossing itself was not straight, it took more of a diagonal path to the other side. The banks were muddy and a crossing line had been marked out with a series of steel posts hammered into the creek bed. I assumed this was the shallowest path. In my direction of travel, I'd also be fighting against the current to get across, which wasn't ideal. I turned off the bike and sat there for a minute, taking it all in. I wasn't about to take any chances.

I had prepared for this very moment, though. Stashed in my saddlebags was a pair of Parramatta footy shorts and a pair of joggers. I stripped off my riding gear, got changed and then waded in. The cold water took my breath away, and it was flowing fast enough to push steadily against my legs. I walked across the crossing several times, looking for the shallowest route. The base was reasonably firm, with a few random rocks scattered underneath.

Back at home I'd measured the height of the air intake on the DR and noted the level on my leg: the mark was just a bit above my knee. If the water was any higher, then my bike would drown. At the deepest point of the crossing, the water level was above my knee but I judged still below my air intake, so I made the decision to cross. To make the job easier, I took all the luggage off my bike:

my saddlebags, fuel bladder, tank bag, the lot. I wanted the bike as light as possible. I could carry the rest of the stuff across later.

I jumped on the bike, started it up and rode to the edge of the creek. I'd made a mental note of where I had walked across the shallowest point and vowed to follow it. I was very nervous—it was now or never.

I rolled into the creek and immediately felt the push of the water against my front wheel—it was strong! Then the whole bike was in and the current pushed hard against the right hand side of the motor and the bottom of the side panels. There was no turning back. I paddled through with my feet down as stabilisers as I kept the engine chugging along in first gear. It felt like I was in there forever. I could see the other side getting closer, but resisted gunning it in case I hit a submerged rock and got thrown off. I stuck close to where I thought my line was, focusing intently on the bank ahead of me. I held the throttle steady with my right hand, while my left hovered over the clutch lever, poised to disengage the clutch if I struck a submerged obstacle. I maintained this steady pace until I got through to the other side and onto the embankment.

I'd made it! Instantly a feeling of elation and relief tore through my body. I let out a loud cry—'Yeah!'—and punched the air, dancing around like a lunatic for a bit. I was letting out all my pent-up worries and it felt great. I was across, and I knew that if I could do this, I could do the rest.

The next thing to think about was my gear. I parked the bike up on the bank and checked the airbox—no water inside, good. Then I crossed back over the creek on foot and did a couple of shuttle runs with my gear. By the time I'd got it all across and repacked, the sun was going down. The adrenaline rush had also worn off and

I was starting to feel the effects of a big day's ride. The only thing left to do was find a campsite.

There was another 30 kilometres along the detour track back to the QAA Line, and I decided that somewhere along there would be my accommodation for the night. I rode into the desert to find somewhere suitable. I must have ridden about ten kilometres or so when I found a nice flat area off the track. The landscape had a green tinge to it, and there were lovely little desert flowers everywhere. It was beautiful.

With less than an hour's light left, I got cracking setting up my camp for the night. I laid down my ground sheet and spread out my tent on top, then stood there and stared at it for a while. It had been a year since I'd last used it, and I had forgotten how to put it up! I'd focused on so many little details as I prepared for this trip, but erecting my tent wasn't one of them.

After twenty minutes or so of fumbling around, it was up. *This has to improve*, I thought to myself, *because I'm not doing this every bloody night*. I got the billy on, made a brew and sat down in my camp chair. This was to be my ritual for the next two weeks. I made dinner and treated myself to my favourite beef teriyaki dehydrated meal, which was delicious.

Today had been a stressful day, but I had overcome what I felt would be my biggest challenge. Now I felt like the ride was really beginning. I slept easily that night, dreaming of the adventure ahead. Three deserts crossed, seven to go.

I'd decided before I left that I wanted to record my thoughts and feelings during the trip. These were the things I wanted to remember long after the aches and pains had been forgotten. On the drive up, I'd purchased a small hardback diary to write in, and it became my companion every night. Beginning tonight, I resolved, I would write something after dinner about the day and how I was feeling.

> Nonstop to my nemesis, the bypass. Put on shorts and runners and waded in to check the depth. Totally unloaded the bike & rode through against the current, rocky and wheel height deep. Walked all my stuff across after. Made it! So happy & no stress now. Bit dehydrated, so drank, ate and sleep time. Looking forward to tomorrow.
>
> Monday, 24 July

7

That's How Accidents Happen

25 July

THIS MORNING, I WOULD RIDE THE EYRE CREEK BYPASS TRACK south before turning west back onto the QAA line into the Northern Territory then turn south aiming for Poeppel Corner, the geographical marker for the intersection of Queensland, the Northern Territory and South Australia. From there I would continue west and spend the majority of the day riding the French Line in South Australia and push myself as far through the Simpson Desert as I could.

I'd never ridden the French Line before, but I'd heard all the stories about how hard it was for motorcyclists—and doubly so for those crazy enough to try it without a four-wheel drive support vehicle. Part of the French Line had been dubbed 'the washing machine'. I wasn't sure why, but I guessed I'd find out soon enough.

The French Line was named after the French petroleum company, which in 1964 was undertaking oil exploration within the Simpson Desert. To facilitate the exploration and the movement of workers and equipment, a road had to be made. It crosses the desert in a more or less straight line running east–west. It's the most popular route chosen by desert explorers as it's the most direct route between the supply stops of Birdsville and Mount Dare. It consists only of two-wheel tracks for hundreds of kilometres, and is considered the hardest crossing of the Simpson Desert due to the deep, soft sand and the enormous dunes.

The conditions are harsh in the Simpson Desert. There is no mobile phone coverage, so satellite communications are a must in the event of an accident or breakdown. The route is only traversable during the cooler winter months, and it's closed during summer as the temperature soars to over 50 degrees Celsius. Those conditions place a huge strain on people and their vehicles, increasing the risk of breakdowns. Recovery services are very limited and expensive. Even in favourable conditions, crossing this desert alone is a big undertaking.

I'd had breakfast and a coffee and my bike was nearly packed. Everything had to be stowed securely, as I knew I would be bouncing around in the dunes all day. The morning was fresh and the skies were clear—perfect riding weather—and I was keen to make a start.

The 30 kilometres along the bypass track back to the QAA Line were uneventful, with a firm dirt track that flowed nicely between the dunes. It was a great way to start the day off, and helped me warm up before the hard stuff began.

Over the years, I've learned a few tips and tricks for riding sand dunes. Firstly, your mindset is crucial: it requires commitment. You need the mental strength to maintain your concentration all day while riding aggressively. Momentum is your friend so you must keep moving: it keeps you high in the soft stuff and stops you from bogging down. You also have to get used to the bike moving around a lot in the sand.

What scares people the most about sand is the instability of the bike, and their inability to control it. But your stability improves with greater momentum, so you must overcome your fear of riding faster in sand. Once you do, you see how much more stable the bike becomes. It tracks straighter and is a lot easier to ride. It gets up and over wheel tracks and tyre marks, rather than digging down into them, which throws you off course. So you have to be aggressive on the throttle. Trust me—it works!

The ride to Poeppel Corner was fairly uneventful. I didn't encounter many other vehicles, so I could brush up on my dune-riding skills. Just after crossing the border from Queensland into the Northern Territory, I took a southerly turn off the QAA line onto the Hay River track. It ran parallel to the dunes and skirted a large dry salt lake, which was fun to ride. The ground was firm and I was able to open up the bike a bit and scoot along at a good pace.

It always makes me chuckle when I see wheel tracks on the edge of a salt lake leading to the middle or taking a short cut—usually the wheels break through the salt crust and the vehicle ends up in the mud beneath. Inevitably this becomes a massive bog hole, from which the vehicle has to be recovered. What were they thinking? I can't imagine how hard it would be to pull a four-wheel drive out of something like that.

•

After heading south for a while, I finally reached Poeppel Corner. Australia has five border corners and Poeppel was my third, as I'd already visited Cameron Corner (at the junction of the borders of Queensland, New South Wales and South Australia) and Haddon Corner (at the north-eastern tip of South Australia). The two remaining on my list are Surveyor Generals Corner (where the borders of Western Australia, the Northern Territory and South Australia meet), and MacCabe Corner (the junction of Victoria, New South Wales and South Australia).

The first thing I noticed when I stopped were the flies. They were thick, buzzing around in my face, my eyes, my nose—bloody everywhere! I hadn't noticed that when riding. After a couple of pictures and a quick look around, I was keen to get my helmet back on and get away from these buzzing pests. From here onward, I would be riding the French Line west in South Australia.

Not long after leaving Poeppel Corner, I had my first encounter with another motorcyclist. I saw a familiar bike outline approaching and realised it was another Suzuki DR650 rider. I pulled up and met Nathan, who was travelling solo from Perth to Melbourne via the Great Central Road and the Simpson Desert. He had been on the road for a little while and was keen to swap stories and chat about the section of the QAA Line he was about to tackle.

I told him that I was trying to break a Guinness World Record, which he thought was really cool, and he was happy to be a witness for my record attempt. I'd never had to prove where I'd ridden before, so I thought it would be a good idea to collect evidence for Guinness World Records to show them where I'd travelled.

We exchanged a few statistics on how much fuel the bikes were using in the sandy conditions so Nathan could be sure he had enough fuel to complete his crossing. We also chatted about the track conditions ahead for both of us. It was great meeting another like-minded traveller, and the sense of camaraderie I felt really lifted my spirits.

The rest of the day gradually got harder and harder. The number of dunes increases as you head west, and many of the approaches up the dune faces were not straight anymore. This necessitated a sharp turn on the deep sandy face before cresting. These were tricky and sapped my energy. A missed gear or too little speed could stop me dead in my tracks, and then I'd be bogged halfway up a dune. I was keen to avoid this situation at any cost. The thought of having to dig the bike out wasn't a pleasant one, so I ensured I carried enough momentum to muscle the heavy bike to the top. Doing this on dune after dune left me exhausted.

I saw a lot more dirt bikers in this section—all were riding lightweight enduro bikes and having a ball. They were out there supported by four-wheel drives that carried their food, fuel and camping gear. I was envious of the ease with which they were carving up the sand as I bounced along like a baby rhinoceros. Now I knew exactly why they called it 'the washing machine'.

By midday the temperature had increased and I was feeling it. My legs were getting tired from all the standing, as were my arms from wrestling with the bike. I was very thirsty, but no matter how much I drank I couldn't quench my thirst. I'd filled my three-litre CamelBak before leaving this morning, adding a few electrolyte tablets, and I was already halfway through it. I stopped at the next little tree I could find and sat in the shade for a while, recovering. I took off my helmet, my head covered in sweat, and felt myself cool down a little. I sat for a while and replenished my energy with some snacks and my favourite sugar jube lollies.

After twenty minutes or so I pushed on. Another hour or so passed and I was in my rhythm again, trying to maintain a steady pace, when I saw a four-wheel drive approaching with an amber beacon flashing on its roof. As I got close, I could see the elderly driver motioning with his hand for me to slow down. Why? Was I approaching an accident? I didn't know.

I slowed as much as I dared, and not long after I came across two elderly ladies with wide-brimmed hats walking across the dunes. They were kitted out with walking poles and hiking gear. Not far behind them was another four-wheel drive with an amber beacon flashing, and as I passed I saw a sign: 'Walkers ahead'. It struck me that they must be walking across the entire Simpson Desert—the crazy things you see out here! What I was doing seemed easy by comparison.

By midafternoon I was getting tired, but I wanted to push on as far as I could to make the next day's riding easier. The washing machine was throwing me all over the bike as I struggled up the twisty dunes for a few more hours. Late that afternoon, though, I started making silly mistakes. I was taking the wrong lines up some of the dunes, which made them harder than they should have been, and I was missing gears when I needed to make quick changes to maintain momentum. I realised I was struggling to maintain the level of concentration required.

It was a sure sign of fatigue. The one positive thing was that I still had a decent level of self-awareness, so I was able to take action. Although the adventurer in me wanted to keep going, my rational self told me to stop before I fell and hurt myself. This was a marathon, not a sprint, I reasoned, and I started looking for a suitable campsite.

The only places to camp in the Simpson Desert are on the flats between the sand dunes, and I was looking for a nice open space devoid of vegetation and pricklies. About an hour and a half before sunset I came across an open claypan and thought,

This is me. I wearily turned the bike to the right and rode onto the claypan. I felt instant relief as the bike left the deep sand. Slowly I rode around the claypan looking for a campsite, like a dog circling before it goes to bed. Eventually I pulled over near the intersection of another track called the Colson Line.

Today had been a good effort. I'd given it everything, which had tested my physical fitness to its limits, so I was glad of all the training I'd done. I was pleased with the distance I'd travelled—about 265 kilometres—and with having made the right decision to stop when I did. The bike had been very heavy to manage all day, with a full load of fuel and supplies, and I was glad to be off it. My arms and legs were sore and I had trouble walking about upright for the first minute or so when I jumped off the bike, wobbling around for a bit.

With my previous night's practice, I had no problem getting the tent erected, and the rest of my camp came together quicker as well. When I finally sat down, I realised that I had drunk nearly all three litres in my CamelBak. Yet I still felt a bit dehydrated. I felt like drinking something other than the orange hydrolyte-flavoured water—I really wanted an iced coffee, but that wasn't going to happen—so I boiled the billy and made up a very sweet cup of coffee. Not the best for hydration, perhaps, but the taste made me feel a lot better. With the remaining water I cooked up another camp meal and managed to scratch a few notes into my diary before falling into a deep sleep.

I hadn't crossed any deserts today—the Simpson is a big one—but tomorrow I would conquer it.

Started riding at 8am, knackered, totally stuffed. Wanted to push on but that's how accidents happen. The dunes on a loaded bike are energy-sapping. Set up camp slowly, better than last night. Waiting for flies to piss off so can have tea.

Tuesday, 25 July

8

Herman and George

26 July

Woke up at 6.30, stiff and sore, legs cramping from yesterday. Can't drink enough.

Wednesday, 26 July

TODAY I WAS AIMING FOR COOBER PEDY. THIS WOULD HAVE ME follow the French Line and complete my crossing of the Simpson Desert. The Pedirka Desert would also be ticked off the list today while finding time for a quick stopover at the Pink Roadhouse.

I hoped I'd crossed the worst of the French Line yesterday—there couldn't be too many dunes left to get over. From previous trips, I knew that the road after Dalhousie Springs all the way to Coober Pedy, my next stop, flattened out, and the surface would change from sand to hard pack and rocks. That would present its own challenges, but it would be less fatiguing than riding in sand. But today promised a long ride, and with the more favourable track conditions I was looking forward to it. I was also still thinking about the iced coffee I'd wished for the night before.

I got back into the familiar rhythm of dune riding: up and down, followed by more up and down. Slowly my body started to warm up, with the stiffness fading away and my arms and legs loosening up. I took it easy at the beginning of the day, as I always enjoy the cool morning air. I like to get the feel of the bike and the terrain before pushing myself harder. I find this gets my mind back in the game, and I start to feel at one with the bike.

It wasn't long before I arrived at Purni Bore and said goodbye to the last of the sand dunes. I had mixed feelings: it was good to see the track firming up, but I was also leaving the remoteness of the Simpson Desert and that sense of isolation and wilderness, which I loved. The French Line had been on my bucket list for many years, and I'd just completed it, unsupported. That in itself was an achievement!

The sand dunes turned into sand corrugations all the way into Dalhousie Springs. The mixture of sand and corrugations required concentration and careful line selection. They're quite different to ride than hard-packed dirt corrugations. Sand corrugations have to be ridden at a reasonable speed to sit on top of the corrugations, but not too fast or you'll vibrate the bike to bits. You also have to watch the ridges made by the four-wheel drives. Crossing those unprepared will snatch the handlebars straight out of your hands and throw you off instantly.

I made sure my steering damper was firm so I could ride over the ridges with confidence, knowing the front wheel would keep tracking straight. I maintained a good pace of 60 to 80 kph all the way to Dalhousie Springs.

I'd been to this oasis in the desert with Farmer only a year before. I didn't have time for a swim, but I could see that there were already morning bathers in there, soaking up the relaxing properties. It was quite a sight, as the cool morning air created a cloud of steam or mist coming up from the warm water. *Next time*, I thought.

I stopped in the main car park, where I saw a large off-road motorhome, the type that sits on a light truck body. It was kitted out with all the luxuries. I needed a rest so I pulled up next to it to have a look, and pretty soon I met Mark, the owner. He and his wife were travelling from Brisbane, doing a loop out across the Simpson Desert, by Uluru and the west MacDonnell Ranges, then back home to Brisbane. His rig had everything you could think of—he and his wife were definitely travelling in style.

I told Mark about how I'd just crossed the Simpson unsupported, and he was surprised when I told him that it was only the start of my Guinness World Record attempt. He thought what I was doing was a great adventure and was more than happy to be another witness for me.

Due to the large amount of rain the region had had in the preceding month, a lot of the roads were still closed, and those that were open were in terrible shape due to overuse. They all had deep wheel ruts, which can catch the unsuspecting motorcycle tyre and spit you off. It was around here that the road also started getting rocky, with some stones the size of large oranges scattered over the surface. Keeping an eye out for them was a constant challenge, as hitting a rock at that speed would mean a fall, a puncture or both.

When riding in the outback, I always run higher tyre pressures. I find it provides insurance against pinch flats when hitting an unexpectedly rough surface or rocks. When you're riding a heavily loaded bike, it can also protect your wheel rims from damage and allow you to ride faster. This approach has worked for me over many outback trips. I was also running a fat-profile front tyre, which provided more sidewall to protect the rim from damage and increased the front footprint of the tyre to help in the sand. I'd used these 'fatty' front tyres before and really liked them. The only downside I noticed was that their width tended to slow down the steering a bit, but I got used to that.

The next desert was the Pedirka, and that would be coming up soon. Located near the south-west corner of the Simpson Desert, this is the smallest desert in Australia that I would be traversing, with a landmass of just 1250 square kilometres. Compare that to the largest Australian desert, the Great Victoria with an area of 348,750 square kilometres, and it really is quite tiny. It's so tiny in fact that I forgot about it, and rode right through without realising!

It must have been getting on for lunchtime, as my stomach was telling me it was time to stop. I found a stand of shady mulga trees and pulled up underneath them. As usual, as soon as I removed my helmet I was greeted by a welcoming committee of annoying little black flies. Lunch for the day was a sachet of tuna and rice, washed down with more orange electrolyte water.

As I was eating, I checked my GPS, as I thought I should have entered the Pedirka Desert by now. Much to my amazement, I found that I had overshot it by 20 kilometres. Bugger! I had wanted to get a picture in each desert, so now I'd have to backtrack after lunch. But it wasn't a major detour, by outback standards.

I rode the 20 kilometres until I found the Pedirka Siding, an abandoned railway siding on the old Ghan line. The old Ghan ran from Port Augusta, in South Australia, all the way to Alice Springs, in the Northern Territory. It was named after the Afghan camel drivers who had helped explore these remote parts of Australia. The Pedirka Siding was used as a watering point for the steam locomotives pulling the old Ghan train. All that was left now was an abandoned building and an old metal railway cart out the front. Still, it was an interesting place to visit and read some of the outback history.

I was taking a photo of my bike in front of the Pedirka Siding sign when a car pulled up behind me. A woman hopped out of the passenger side, and almost immediately after her came a brown Burmese cat. I walked over to say hello and noticed there was another brown Burmese stretched out sunning himself on the dashboard of their four-wheel drive. It's not every day you see that!

Sue and her husband, Les, had been travelling around the outback with their two chocolate-brown Burmese cats, Herman and George. The cats were quite accustomed to car travel and liked to lie on the dashboard or on the passenger's lap. Sue took Herman for a walk to stretch his legs, and he wandered around like an obedient dog, never straying too far and coming back when called. I'd never seen such a well-trained cat. Sue and Les had travelled from Brisbane to Maralinga, and were now meandering home.

I explained to Sue what I was doing and she was kind enough to witness my crossing of the Pedirka Desert. I really enjoyed chatting to her and Les and hearing about their trip—these encounters are what makes adventures like this all the more interesting.

Having added 40 kilometres to my day's ride, I said my goodbyes and took off in a cloud of dust. My next stop was another place I'd visited before: the famous Pink Roadhouse. It was only a hundred kilometres or so to Oodnadatta, and I covered it relatively quickly, arriving in the early afternoon. I topped up my long-range fuel tank and picked up a large iced coffee as well. I found a seat outside and drank it slowly, savouring the flavour.

The Pink Roadhouse was unseasonably quiet, with no other travellers around. On my previous visits it had always been a hive of activity, with vehicles buzzing around, the petrol pumps whirring and people flocking to the cafe. I enjoyed my iced coffee in the peace and quiet, half-expecting to see a tumbleweed blowing down the street in front of me.

The ride from Oodnadatta to Coober Pedy was the easiest so far. It was a wide, graded dirt road, and it was here that I longed for the legs of my KTM 990 Adventure S. The DR still had the shorter gearing on it from the Simpson crossing, which limited my top speed, but I couldn't be bothered changing it again. I cruised along in the afternoon sun, with my favourite country music playing into my helmet—life was good. Suddenly this didn't seem like a Guinness World Record attempt at all!

•

Arriving at Coober Pedy, I saw the familiar moonscape and muck heaps around the edge of the town. Coober Pedy is opal-mining territory and the muck heaps are large mounds of dirt excavated from underground mining operations. It's a bit of a wild west town, comprised of many small claims with people looking to strike it lucky and make their fortune. I wondered how many actually had. It's also something of a lifestyle choice: plenty of people there are escaping the rat race of the cities and trying something new. They're a very eclectic bunch in Coober Pedy, but always welcoming.

I'd decided to treat myself to a motel room for this night. I knew the next leg of the trip was going to be tough, so I wanted to be well rested. The Mud Hut Motel was a familiar place having stayed there the previous year, so I knew I'd be comfortable. This was also the first of my two resupply points. I'd posted a box full of ration packs to the Coober Pedy Post Office, which would keep me going until I reached my next resupply point, in Western Australia.

After I checked in, I unloaded what I needed and then commenced my daily routine of checking over the bike. I'd made sure to do a thorough visual inspection of the bike at the end of each day, to make sure nothing was broken or damaged from the day's riding. I also checked things like the chain tension, the wheel nuts and the tyre condition. I don't lubricate the chain on rides like this, as the sand would only stick to the lube and do more damage than good. I always use the best quality XW Ring chains, and had fitted a new one before leaving. I knew from experience that it would last the entire distance without needing attention—preventative maintenance! Looking after the bike before I looked after myself made me feel better. I'm not sure why, but I just did it.

When I was happy the bike was good to go for the next day, I took care of myself. A shower, a change of clothes and off to the pub! I ate a big steak dinner that night—it would be my last for a few weeks.

I'd ridden over 500 kilometres today, and had officially crossed five deserts now—halfway! But the big deserts were coming.

Caught up with messages and phoned home. Certainly makes it easier with this many people looking out for me!

Wednesday, 26 July

9

Pushing On

27 July

It was to be a simple day today, head west for Western Australia and ride as far as I could through the Great Victoria Desert.

It was early morning in Coober Pedy when I got up. The forecast showed fine weather for the day ahead, albeit a little chilly at first.

I love these multi-day rides into the outback, with just the road ahead of me and my bike underneath, exploring off the beaten track. They really excite me. All the daily worries of life and work are forgotten as I can just focus on what lies beyond. I'm sure other riders can relate. On a motorcycle, you live in the moment, more so than when you're driving a car, I reckon. You smell the air, feel the rain or the heat and experience everything first-hand.

My next leg was along the Anne Beadell Highway, where Farmer and I had ridden the previous year. Now I was heading in the opposite direction, though, and I was alone, which would make me a little more cautious as I knew how remote and rough the track was.

I rode over to the truck stop on the edge of town and filled my main fuel tank with 36 litres and one fuel bladder with 12 litres. If all things went to plan, I would be riding for two days until my next fuel stop at the remote roadhouse of Ilkurlka some 800 kilometres away. Along with the additional fuel load I topped up my water reserves to ten litres of water. I was travelling into very remote country now and had to cater for all eventualities. This made for a heavy bike. The weight was well spaced out, though, with the fuel in the front and rear, and the water in the middle of my saddlebags. The modified suspension handled it easily and the bike sat level at the fuel bowser.

This was my last opportunity for a decent coffee for a while, so I grabbed one and paired it with a delicious bacon and egg roll—staple bikers' food. When I was finished, I pointed my bike west and headed back out into the desert.

The stretch of the Anne Beadell Highway between Coober Pedy and Emu Field has the worst corrugations in all of Australia. I'm convinced of it. Of all the rough dirt tracks, backroads and goat trails I've ridden, no other comes close to the tedious corrugations on this awful section. There are approximately 250 kilometres in this section, all the way out to the Emu Field atomic test site, where the surface is hard ironstone gravel making the corrugations sharp and very tall.

Corrugations were the terrain that worried me the most, as they could easily damage my bike due to the extreme vibrations and constant pounding on the suspension. Ride too slow and I could sink into them and get badly shaken about; ride too fast and I could lose control. It was the 'Goldilocks speed' I was after, not too fast and not too slow.

Having mechanical sympathy for your equipment is a must. You have to understand how your bike is reacting to the conditions, and stay aware of the punishment it's taking. You need to know when it's becoming too much and adjust your speed or your riding line. Failure to do so can result in an accident or damage to your bike. This constant mental processing of terrain and bike is a big part of what makes a long-distance ride exhausting.

These sorts of conditions were foremost in my mind when I was planning how I would carry all my gear on this trip. Anything bolted to the bike—such as hard panniers—wouldn't last due to the constant vibrations so I'd chosen the saddlebag option. My saddlebags were slung across the seat and were unaffected by the road conditions, insulated by the suspension and able to move with the bike.

My main concern was the long-range fuel tank and the weight it carried when full. The tank is so big it requires a cross brace at the front to prevent it from splaying outwards and falling off the frame mounts. This aluminium brace has been known to rub on the cylinder head and break. If that happened, the tank would drop down and almost touch the engine. I was carrying a spare tank brace for this reason, and I kept a close eye on things. The corrugations shook the tank to death all day, but it stood up to the punishment, which was a testament to its design and strength.

It was around this time, though, that I started feeling some numbness in my hands. The constant harsh vibrations through the handlebars were affecting them, making it hard to hold onto the handlebars. After an hour of riding I had to stop to regain feeling, which wasn't ideal. But I knew that the surface would improve after Emu Field, so I persevered.

I alternated my riding position, standing up for a while and then sitting down, so I could give different muscles in my body a rest. I was always on the lookout for a smoother line. Some parts of the road had what's known as a 'chicken track', where someone has made a new track off at the side. The chicken tracks begin smoother than the originals but over time they become just as corrugated.

In some sections there were three or four chicken tracks, and choosing the best one was becoming a sport.

The vibrations were relentless all morning, as I skated over awful ironstone ridges that varied from five centimetres to nearly 15 centimetres in height. The bike was getting pounded and the suspension was working hard, moving up and down sharply. If something was going to break, this would be the place. When the vibration became too much, I would slow right down and change my line. Thankfully I got through the worst of it with no damage to my bike.

This time when I reached Emu Field, there was no exploring like the previous year. It was around lunchtime, so I stopped at the same spot we'd camped the year before. I sat in a shady spot eating my tuna and reminiscing about the good time I'd had here with Farmer. It was quiet, with no breeze and a cool, cloudy sky, and I hadn't seen another person all morning. Just me and my bike.

I savoured the solitude while I ate and overlooked the large red Emu Field claypan. Once again I found my mind turning back to the days when planes would have been landing here, the area abuzz with activity. After lunch I emptied my fuel bladder into the main tank. With the bladder now empty, a substantial weight would be removed from the rear of the bike improving its handling. After I stowed everything away, the silence was broken by the familiar *bop, bop, bop* of the big thumper as I continued on.

Not far after Emu Field, the track became sandy again. The twin wheel tracks smoothed out a little, but another obstacle presented itself: 'slappy sticks'. These are the tree branches that grow right to the side of the wheel tracks in which I was riding. There were various tree types along the desert tracks, and as the four-wheel drives push through, they break off the branches at the track's edge.

But a motorbike riding in the four-wheel drive's tracks has handlebars that are wider than the wheels, so the branches constantly slap the bike like a whip. If you ride in the left wheel track, your left arm gets constantly whipped by the slappy sticks and will end up quite badly bruised. Trust me, it's painful!

Another issue is that larger-diameter sticks that aren't quite as flexible as the smaller ones can catch on your handlebar and deflect your steering. Not ideal! So this required constant attention and good judgement. I also had to think of the luggage I was carrying, especially my precious water and fuel—if a stick pierced any of those containers I would suddenly have a very big problem.

As much as possible, I chose to ride in the left-hand wheel track when there were slappy sticks around, as the DR is fitted with a rectangular oil cooler on its right-hand side. A hole in that would cause even bigger problems. I judged that it was better to have a bruised arm than a busted oil cooler.

The only other option was to ride in the middle of the track, but that came with its own dangers. The sand there was much deeper sand, and was scattered with spinifex shrubs that love to puncture tyres. If you choose to ride in the middle, you have to ride faster to stay straight in the deep sand, but you risk being bounced off by a spinifex shrub into the slappy sticks. Sounds like fun, hey? I kept this up for hours on end, power on, power off, ricocheting from one side of the track to the other.

•

As I rode the Anne Beadell Highway, I moved through different types of terrain. First there were the ironstone corrugations and open country with low-level shrubbery enabling you to see for miles, then the sandy, slappy stick country, which closed in on you, tightening your focus. Finally the landscape opened up again into sand dunes and sand ridge country. Sand ridges are like sand dunes, just smaller—nothing like the dunes of the French Line.

The track flowed nicely now, over and sometimes around the sand ridges, a bit like a roller-coaster. I was able to maintain a decent pace through this section, as the vegetation trackside had really opened up. It was great fun, and not too taxing on either me or the bike.

I rode like this until the late afternoon, when again the terrain changed and the sand ridges began to flatten out. I was starting to think about how much longer I'd ride and began looking out for a suitable place to camp. As strong as the temptation was to push on and ride into the night, I wasn't going to break my rule—the risks were too great.

Camp selection is not a chore to be taken lightly—at least not by me! I'm fussy when it comes to where I'm stopping for the night. It must be a nice, flat, open area, not under trees, with a supply of wood, and with a view if possible. Some sort of natural shelter from the wind is also nice. That's not too much to ask, is it?

A few kilometres down the track, a nice turn-out appeared on the right-hand side. It backed onto a sand ridge, which provided shelter from the wind, and there was ample firewood for the night. Perfect.

That evening I cooked my dinner and took it up to the top of the nearby sand ridge. The view was stunning. I could see for kilometres across Australia's largest desert, the Great Victoria, and out into the remoteness of Central Australia. I hadn't seen a soul all day—what an amazing feeling. I wondered whether this was how the early colonial explorers felt.

I watched the sun set and felt its warmth leave me as the darkness of night took over, then I made my way back to my little yellow tent for a well-earned rest.

I was well into my sixth desert, having travelled about 400 kilometres today. I was pleased with that effort—and, more importantly, my bike and I were still unscathed.

> Haven't seen anyone since leaving Coober Pedy. Saw three busted camper trailers, two abandoned, and one waiting repairs. Also saw a metal chainguard from a Yamaha T7. The corrugations are horrendous.
>
> Thursday, 27 July

10

Getting It Done

28 July

I WAS STILL IN THE GREAT VICTORIA DESERT, AND THE ISOLATION of my overnight stop was one of my best camp experiences. I would remain in the Great Victoria Desert today, hopefully making Ilkurlka.

Another good sleep: with all the hard riding, I didn't stir all night.

To minimise the chances of unwanted night-time visitors of the furry kind, I followed a particular camp etiquette. Every night before bed, I made sure all my foodstuffs were packed up, empty meal packs stuffed into the rubbish bag and sealed up, all the lids back on my water containers, my CamelBak stowed either on my bike or in the tent with me, and the saddlebags strapped up. The duffel bag that contained my camping equipment went under the tent's vestibule, along with my riding boots. I'd then do a general clean-up to make sure there were no food scraps left anywhere near my tent. All this was to discourage dingoes or other animals from getting into my rations or generally being a nuisance at night.

I also made sure that all toileting took place some distance away from camp, with a hole dug for number twos. This both stopped the smells from attracting animals and prevented unsightly toilet paper from blowing around in the bush.

I like routines. Doing things the same way minimises mistakes, stops you forgetting things and generally promotes a better outcome. I packed my bike the same way each morning. Every item had its place, and always went back where it came from. Each strap was tied down the way it had been. This made packing up quicker, and assured me that I wouldn't lose anything.

After packing, I'd pull and prod all my luggage to make sure it was secure. I'd also have a general look over the bike again to make sure everything seemed right. This was one part of my daily preparation that I never rushed.

The terrain started off the same as the day before, a sandy but open twin track, fluctuating with more closed sections and slappy sticks. The bike felt good but I noticed a couple of squeaking sounds coming from the front end. I was riding easily, warming everything up, so I decided to monitor the new noises to see if they went away. Further down the track, I saw a couple of four-wheel drives approaching. It was a long, straight section that was very narrow and overgrown where we were going to meet, so I pulled off the track to give them space to pass me. The first vehicle stopped, and that was when I met Rod and his wife.

They, along with their two friends, who were in the vehicle behind, were on the last leg of their Northern Territory and Western Australian trip. Their vehicles were well set up with rooftop tents and fridges full of steak and beer—things I could only dream of! They commented on how overgrown the track was and showed me the scratches all along the sides of their vehicles from the slappy sticks. They were amazed that I was managing to ride through. Rod was also a DR rider and keen to hear about how I set up my bike to cope with the conditions and the extra weight.

As I was talking to Rod, I felt that my back was wet so I took off my CamelBak and found it had been leaking. I'd lost a fair bit of water and hadn't noticed it when riding along. I checked the

CamelBak for leaks but couldn't find any, so I topped it up from one of the water bottles in my saddlebag, screwed the lid back on tight and hoped for the best. Rod offered to replace the water I'd used from my water bottle, but I had plenty so there was no need. I love the generosity of folks when you're out in the bush, it's like an unwritten rule to help out a fellow traveller if needed. Rod and I exchanged details, and I now had a witness for my Great Victorian Desert crossing. With a smile and a wave, Rod and his friends went trundling along eastward as I continued west.

Before riding off, I made an adjustment to my steering damper: I wanted to firm it up a little. While turning the adjusting knob, I noticed it was a little more resistant than usual. I moved the handlebar from left to right and heard a creaking sound coming from the steering head stem/damper area. My mind started racing. Did I have a problem with my steering damper? Had the desert sand and corrugations broken something inside it? Had the oil inside the damper broken down? If my damper broke, my ride could be over. Should I go on or turn back? I was, after all, over 500 kilometres away from any mechanical assistance.

I tend to overthink problems sometimes, which can be a problem in itself. This ride wasn't only a test of machine but also of man, and my mental resilience to setbacks. I was aware of this, so made a concerted effort to think the issue through and trust in my preparations. I said to myself: *You've prepared everything you can, you have enough tools, food, water and communications equipment to cover everything. Trust yourself and get on with it.*

I rode on, and the squeaking and creaking seemed to get worse, although I didn't notice any change in the performance of the steering damper. It was then I noticed that the small windscreen

I had fitted to the DR's headlight cowl had shifted a little. It was sitting back on the right-hand side, and appeared to be moving around more than it should. I stopped again.

Once stationary, I grabbed hold of the top of the windscreen and gave it a tug. *Squeak*. I wobbled it again: *squeak*. Now I was getting somewhere. I got off the bike and took a close look at the aluminium brackets that I had fabricated at home to support the windscreen at high speed. They were bent at a 90-degree angle and mounted to the Barkbusters hand guards. One of them had broken due to the constant vibration. I wobbled the screen again, heard the squeak and saw the aluminium bracket rubbing on the hand guard. Ha! Squeak number one located.

I dived into my trusty tool kit and pulled out an essential that everyone should carry—cable ties. I tied the screen tightly and trimmed the ends. Now the screen was fixed securely and wouldn't move or squeak anymore. I was happy.

I sat on the bike and moved the handlebars left and right, and the creaking sound was still there. This was definitely coming from the steering and the damper area. I felt better after identifying and fixing one simple problem, but the possibility of a steering damper failure troubled me. I decided to push on and monitor the sound and the feel of the steering.

The country changed again as I moved out of the sandy slappy sticks and back onto hard ironstone and rocks. It was good to get away from the constant tree branches brushing up against me, but now I had to focus on avoiding sharp rocks and severe corrugations.

Along the way I came to a dry salt lake, where the view opened up a bit. I stopped for morning tea, which consisted of a muesli bar and some sugar jube lollies. It was great to have a bit of elevation again and look across the dry lake bed, imagining what the country would be like if it were in flood. For one thing, I could see that the track would be cut in wet weather, as it went straight through the lake bed. Again, the remoteness of the place was clear: there was nothing as far as the eye could see.

I also noticed that my CamelBak was still leaking. Damn! I inspected it for rips or tears in the bladder but saw nothing. I was stumped. I refilled it from my water container and was screwing down the lid again when I noticed that the O-ring at the base of the thread was twisting if I screwed the lid on too tight. This time, therefore, I didn't screw it on as tightly. Maybe I'd crimped the O-ring last time? I was hoping that was what it was, as I couldn't afford to lose much more water to leaks.

I knew from my previous year's trip that on the other side of the dry salt lake, all the way to my intended overnight location of Ilkurlka, there were twisty, undulating sand dunes. They went for another 250 kilometres, so it would be hard riding if I was to make it there by day's end.

•

One of the great sights—and smells—in the outback are the feral camels. There are thousands of them scattered across Central Australia. They generally travel in herds, with a number of females and one larger male camel, or bull. A bull camel stands at over two metres tall at the hump and weighs over 800 kilograms, so they are not to be messed with. I'd seen them in this section the year before and so was keeping a good lookout as I starting cresting the dunes again.

The country surrounding the track was thick mulga scrub. The track that cut through the scrub was the smoothest pathway for animals to travel along, so it naturally became a highway for them too. I started seeing camel footprints, which are unmissable due to their large, roundish shape. In fact, their prints can be quite useful when you're riding. The camels are smart enough to use the smoothest part of the track and will avoid the worst corrugations, so it usually pays to follow in their footprints.

After a while I noticed more camel tracks, and it wasn't long before I encountered a large bull camel walking along in front of me. His harem of females walked off into the bush but this big guy was having none of it, and he continued along in front of me.

I'd experienced this before, and had been held up for kilometres behind a pacing camel. I approached to about five metres behind the big beast, and it was there that I got a good whiff of it. The stink! I started tooting the DR's horn to encourage him to move off the track.

With me behind, the camel started pacing along in the left-side wheel track at about 25 kph, and I was following the same line as I tooted away, but he just looked over his left shoulder and refused to budge. So I moved over to the right-side track and tooted again, hoping to encourage him into the bush on his left. No—now the camel moved into the right wheel track, blocking me. I moved back to the left, tooted, and then the camel moved left too.

By now I was getting a serious case of road rage! I think the camel was as well, as it was foaming at the mouth and thighs. He was getting quite worked up, and the foam started coming off the big beast, spraying onto me. Not only was the smell disgusting but now I was getting covered in its bodily fluids! I couldn't bear this for much longer.

This little game went on for a few hundred metres until I decided to overtake. I had never done this before, though, so I wasn't sure how I would go. There was no room for me to take a wide berth around, so I would have to overtake in the open wheel track, which was only a metre from its side. I didn't like the idea but saw little other option.

I practised changing wheel tracks a couple of times, without tooting the horn. To my surprise, the camel didn't move over as quickly. Obviously, camels are unpredictable, though, so that still didn't give me much confidence. Finally I garnered enough courage to have a go.

I waited until there was a straight stretch of track and the sand ridge in the middle wasn't too deep. I made sure I was in second gear, with plenty of punch available. It was now or never. I jumped from the left wheel track into the right and gunned it past the big fella. My heart was in my mouth—one rightward step and nearly a ton of stinking hairy camel could barge me off my bike.

I drew alongside him and was just ahead of his shoulder when he swung his big head around to look at me. Here we go, I thought, I'm about to get trampled! But then he stepped off the track to the left and away into the bush. I'd made it!

My heart was racing. I'd taken a big risk, I realised, and fortunately it had paid off. I made a mental note to keep my camel rage in check and not be as impatient next time.

•

I spent the rest of the day riding the roller-coaster of sand dunes and ridges. At some point I crossed into Western Australia, but I didn't know exactly when as there was no marker post welcoming me in. I'd made good time, pushing hard all day, and was sure I'd make Ilkurlka that afternoon. In fact, I'd cut a whole day off my previous travel time between Coober Pedy and Ilkurlka, so I was feeling very pleased with myself. Approximately 800 kilometres in two days, and I was feeling it.

I had pre-booked fuel and lodgings, because I knew I'd want a hot shower and comfy bed tonight. How glad I was to have made those arrangements when I pulled into the Ilkurlka roadhouse.

This time, when I arrived, I was met by Alex, a young bloke who was filling in while the regular caretaker, Phil, was on leave. Alex told me his parents had met when they were working at Tjuntjuntjara, the nearest Indigenous community, and he reckons he took his first steps at Ilkurlka. He was a typical country kid, laid-back, relaxed and not in a hurry to do anything. We spent a while chatting before he took me over to the shed to fuel up my bike.

All the fuel at Ilkurlka is in drums that are brought on a truck from Laverton, about 600 kilometres to the west. It has to be booked in advance so they can determine how many drums to put on the truck for each delivery. Opal fuel, which is the only petrol available in a lot of outback regions, is generally kept in lesser quantities than diesel at Ilkurlka, as the majority of vehicles run on diesel fuel in the bush. Opal is standard 91-octane unleaded petrol but doesn't have the smell like normal petrol. It's made like that to prevent petrol sniffing, which is a real health issue. I'd used this type of fuel plenty of times before and knew it would be fine for my bike.

I'd reserved 50 litres—at a cost of $5 per litre—so I was able to fill up my tank and fuel bladder. Alex used a very old hand pump to transfer the fuel out of the drum and into a big glass filter, then it flowed through an old black hose into my petrol tank. Most of the fittings on the pump leaked profusely and the filter looked pretty dirty, so I wondered how much clean fuel I was getting for my money. Thankfully, I had fitted filters on my fuel lines to cope with the dirt I was expecting from drum fuel.

Next I rode up to the overnight accommodation, which was an aluminium donga perched on top of a sand ridge. The front verandah had a great view out into the desert country and towards the setting sun. All the colours of the desert come alive in the afternoon with the softening light. I just wanted to sit down and stare into space for a while, but I couldn't. I had jobs that needed attention.

First and foremost was checking over the bike before it got too dark. I unpacked what I needed, which wasn't much as I wasn't camping tonight. I gave the bike a good visual inspection, then checked the oil level, the chain tension, the spokes, the brackets and the nuts and bolts. I looked for any cracks in the frame or damage to anything else. Once I was happy that the bike was okay, I looked at the steering again. It was making that creaking sound when I moved the handlebars left and right, but there was still a decent amount of resistance from the steering damper.

It had me stumped—the damper was still working, and all the fittings were tight and undamaged. I decided to leave it be, as there was nothing I could do about it now anyway.

I was keen for a wash, so I went out the back and lit a fire under the donkey shower. In about fifteen minutes, the water was hot enough for a nice warm shower. I washed myself and did some laundry, hoping it would dry by tomorrow morning.

Tonight, I had the place all to myself—no floor for me this time! The pull-out bed was comfy and it wasn't long after dinner that it was lights-out.

Corrugations are seriously nasty, bike was light—low fuel—low water got to Ilkurlka a day early. Donkey shower and bed—luxury. I was worried about squeaking noise, tend to catastrophise things, played on my mind. I hate being nervous, but I'm getting it done. Have to be so careful out here. In saying that, got impatient & overtook a camel. Bloody thing wouldn't move. Never again, scary.

Friday, 28 July

11

Amazing but Dangerous

29 July

My journey today would take me on a more northerly trajectory. I would ride out of the Great Victoria Desert and camp up somewhere in the neighbouring Gibson Desert tonight.

If you ever get the chance to travel deep into Central Australia, you have to visit Ilkurlka and stay overnight. There are camping spots there as well as the accommodation I used, and it's well worth the effort of getting there. The next morning I spoiled myself by lying in bed and watching the sun rise over the red sandhills of the Great Victoria Desert and light up the surrounding country. The view out the front window was so good, and I was so comfortable, that for a while I forgot about what I was doing. It almost felt like a normal day at home.

Eventually I dragged myself out of the cosy donga and got stuck into my morning routines of packing, checking and checking again. For some reason I was feeling wary this morning. Was it because I was leaving the relative comforts of Ilkurlka and heading back out into the great unknown? Or was it the squeaking noises on my bike? I wasn't sure.

As part of my training regime for this ride, I had made an effort to prepare myself mentally for the adverse situations and setbacks that I might confront. I wanted to toughen myself up in the face of fatigue, breakdowns, accidents and the apprehensiveness I sometimes feel when travelling solo in remote areas. Time and time again I have got myself out of situations in the outback where I've broken down or fallen off, so I knew I was capable physically, but I was aware that I worried about things unnecessarily. I wanted to remedy that.

I'd never been one for self-help books or life coaches or that type of thing—it just wasn't my style. I found that stuff too warm and fuzzy. But one day I was browsing through social media when I came across a page set up by a former US Navy Seal, David Goggins. He was now a motivational speaker, also an author who had released a book titled *Can't Hurt Me*, and his ideas interested me. There was something about his delivery, too, that resonated with me: it was real, it was based on his life experiences and to me it made sense. I read his book as I was keen to hear his thoughts on how to develop mental toughness in adverse situations, as I felt I could adopt them in my life.

I listened to him when I was riding my bike around Lake Burley Griffin, visualising endless punishing sand dunes, and when I was hiking alone, comparing the solitude of the bush I was in to the solitude of the desert I would be traversing. This certainly had a positive effect on me and my riding: it gave me a more positive mindset and strengthened my ability to cope in the face of adversity. I had already noted how this mindset had helped me when I crossed the Simpson Desert and I was exhausted. I would use it again and again for other parts of this ride as well.

This morning, to overcome my wariness, I adopted a mantra I had heard Goggins use many times. *Stay hard*, I repeatedly said to myself. It was time for me to sharpen my focus on the day ahead.

Today I would continue heading west on the Anne Beadell Highway to Neale Junction before taking a northerly turn onto the Connie Sue Highway towards the town of Warburton, about

500 kilometres away. I wasn't expecting to make it all the way there today, but I wanted to push hard to get as close as I could. I knew the next 200 or so kilometres west were not too bad, as I had ridden it the year before, but it was the turn north on the Connie Sue Highway that was the great unknown.

I'd ridden the southern part of the Connie Sue and it had been rough. From travel reports I'd read and research I'd undertaken, apparently the northern section was in worse condition. Wow! How much worse could it be? It made me a little uneasy as to what lay ahead.

The ride westward to Neale Junction was more corrugated, sandy tracks with some small sandhills thrown in for good measure. The conditions were taking their toll and my body was sore again almost from the start. My left hand and wrist were aching from the constant vibration of the handlebars over the corrugations, and my neck and knees were sore as well. I stopped a few times that morning for snacks, and for the first time wrote in my diary during the day, trying to remember as much as I could.

> Constantly tensing for deep sand, fourth gear 65 kph, brutal! Concentration hard, ever-changing track, sand/deep sand/ruts/corrugations/gravel. Differing colours, dark coloured corrugations the worst. Always searching for smoothest path at speed very tiring.
>
> Saturday, 29 July

Maintaining a fast enough pace made riding the sand easier, but it also increased the speed at which I had to make decisions on line selection. I couldn't rest for a second: I was always analysing the terrain ahead, moving the bike to smoother lines and dodging obstacles.

It was always a balance between riding fast enough but not dangerously. It can be easy to get carried away through a fun section and to let your speed increase, but I never pushed myself to 100 per cent of my skill level, to ensure that I always had something in reserve in case of emergency. The squeaking in the front end was still there but hadn't got any worse, so I just kept an ear on it. The steering didn't feel any different, so I wasn't overly worried. I placed faith in my preparation, and also in the equipment I'd chosen to do its job.

•

I arrived at Neale Junction around lunchtime, ready for a break. I'd been there before but now I was heading in a new direction. I pulled up near the big silver container right in the middle of the intersection, which contained the visitors' book. I wanted to check it to see if my entry from the year before was still there—sure enough, there it was! I read the comment Farmer and I had left, which perked me up a bit as I remembered the good times we'd shared travelling through here. I relaxed a little as I looked northwards, up the Connie Sue, and saw the little brown strip of track which would lead me out of the Great Victoria Desert and into the Gibson Desert.

After a quick bite to eat, I entered the northern section of the Connie Sue Highway. I'd been riding along at a steady pace, getting a feel for the new track, when I saw a LandCruiser approaching from the opposite direction. As I was the smaller vehicle, I moved off to the side of the track, and I watched as it pulled up next to me.

Out of the driver's seat climbed Andrew, followed by his wife, Michelle, who were keen to say g'day. They'd been travelling the outback for some years and so were seasoned travellers, having driven most of the tracks made by Len Beadell. Even though most of the tracks were in poor condition, Andrew reckoned, they took them to more interesting places—a sentiment with which I agreed wholeheartedly.

Andrew was also a rider, and—would you believe it—had a DR650 as well. It just goes to show how popular these bikes are. Instantly we were like two old friends, swapping bike stories and ride reports from previous trips. Michelle listened patiently as we raved on like long-lost friends. Andrew told me about his adventure to Cape York on his DR, while I explained my current adventure. They were eager to be a part of my journey and signed up as two more witnesses for Guinness World Records.

Ironically, Andrew had commented to Michelle just before we met that the Connie Sue would be a bastard to ride on a motorbike, due to the slappy sticks and the soft, sandy centre ridge. I agreed, and we had a chuckle about that.

It was great meeting Andrew and Michelle—it gave me a real boost of energy for the afternoon's ride. I had another three hours of daylight left, so had to make the most of it and get as close to Warburton as I could.

The track conditions deteriorated, though, with the introduction of deep ironstone gravel. It's like sand but made up of small particles of gravel, and the bike would sink right in if I rode too slowly. The ridges and ruts of this stuff were harder to cross, though, and really grabbed hold of my front wheel. Riding took maximum concentration and effort all afternoon, as the trackside foliage got thicker and the slappy sticks came back. It was a real challenge just to stay upright.

> *Hard going, deep, deep ironstone sand and gravel ruts with close trees hitting handlebars. Max concentration 30–40 kph.*
>
> *Saturday, 29 July*

I was concentrating so hard that I barely got to look at the countryside I was in. I'd ridden out of the Great Victoria Desert, which had taken me three days, and had now moved into the Gibson Desert. It all looked the same to me.

About an hour before I stopped for the night, the track was getting corrugated again and I saw the display on my GPS flickering: it had started alternating from 12-volt power to battery power for some reason. I had a Garmin Rino 750 on a rubber RAM mount on the handlebars to dampen the vibrations. The Rino was a good unit that also incorporated a UHF radio that I connected to speakers in my helmet via a Bluetooth connection. I used a 'push to talk' button mounted on the handlebars that enabled me to speak with four-wheel drives as I rode. It was plugged into a USB accessory plug I had fitted to the handlebars with rubber mounts, which was powered by the bike's auxiliary power circuit. It had been working flawlessly since I left Marree, so I wasn't sure what might have gone wrong.

I pulled over and had a look at all the connections first. The cable into the back of the GPS was secure and firm. At the other end of the cable, where it plugged into the USB charger, it was looser and moved around a bit. I turned the bike key on so the USB charger had power and wiggled the cable in it, which caused the GPS to flick into and out of battery mode. The constant vibrations of the corrugations had evidently caused some wear in the USB charger port.

What to do? Cable ties! I grabbed some more from my tool kit and tied them around the charging cable, and then tied that around the USB charger so it pulled the cable in tight to the charging port. I turned the power on again and tried to wiggle the cable, which didn't move. Problem solved—cable ties to the rescue again.

•

I rode until about half an hour before sunset. Dusk, like dawn, is a dangerous time to ride in the Australian outback: the wildlife is a lot more active and the chances of an animal strike increase dramatically. I found a little turn-out on the left-hand side of the track, with a nice, flat, open area for me to set up my tent.

I did that in record time, as I wanted to go for a little wander before sunset. I'd noticed some interesting rock formations behind my camp that warranted closer inspection. So, in my paper-thin thongs, I gingerly set off across a carpet of sharp ironstone pebbles. Not far behind my camp I located a dry creek bed with a very steep bank—it was more like a little gorge. I could see that in the other side of the bank there were some small caves that had been used as a campsite. It looked like there had been a natural hole in the rock, which had been excavated to create a smooth, flat floor for sleeping. Inside I noticed grey ash where fires had been set.

As I wandered along this little gorge, I saw more and more caves in the side of the bank, and wondered whether at some point in time they had been inhabited by Indigenous people of this area.

It was amazing to be in this barren, rough landscape and to think of people living in the caves. The creek bed was bone-dry; it must only flow when the rains allowed it to, in the wetter months.

The surrounding countryside was very rocky, which made it hard to navigate in my rubber thongs, so I didn't climb down the embankment for a closer look. What footwear could the people who had lived here have used, I wondered. Their feet must have been tough! I wondered whether this had been a home base or just a shelter for nomadic people.

I thought I had stumbled on something amazing, and I took a lot of pictures but didn't venture any closer. This seemed like something few outsiders had seen, and very special. I walked the creek a little more before heading back to my camp before sunset.

That little discovery really made my day. I'd ridden nearly 400 kilometres and had completed my sixth desert, but it was fantastic to take my mind off riding for a while.

> *Great camp about 100 kilometres south of Warburton; isolation is amazing but dangerous. Gorge really cool, took pics. Bike's running well, listened to some John Williamson at dinnertime, feeling content and ready for bed. Another big push tomorrow.*
>
> *Saturday, 29 July*

12

Dreaming

30 July

I WOULD SPEND THE DAY IN THE GIBSON DESERT, MAKING A westerly track onto the Gunbarrel Highway. My aim was to cover as much distance as I could on Gunbarrel Highway and make camp overnight somewhere along it.

I woke up with a spring in my step as I knew I'd be venturing into Warburton today. It was familiar territory to me, which meant I could relax a little as I knew what to expect. I hoped that would allow me to cover a decent distance as well. It also meant that I would be at a roadhouse today and so could eat some greasy food and drink an iced coffee. I was looking forward to that!

I would have loved to explore the gorge I'd discovered during daylight hours, but unfortunately I couldn't spare the time. *Maybe another time*, I said to myself, but I knew deep down that I'd likely never be back there again.

The ride into Warburton was much better than the riding yesterday as the track improved a lot, providing a hard surface instead of the usual sand. Thankfully, there was less trackside shrubbery too, and consequently I made good time, with the Warburton roadhouse welcoming me at about 9.30am.

The Warburton roadhouse is the town hub, providing a supermarket for the community and an essential stopover for travellers crossing the continent along the Great Central Road (GCR). The GCR is an 1100-kilometre stretch of dirt road between Laverton, in Western Australia, and Yulara, in the Northern Territory. It was a ride I'd completed a few years before on my KTM 990 Adventure S, and at that time I hadn't thought it was that great due to the endless corrugations.

Most of the main outback roads are looked after by the local councils, which have a yearly grading schedule to maintain their road network. Most dirt roads get an annual grading if they're lucky. Travel the road after the grader's been on it and it's smooth sailing; unfortunately, I reckon I'd ridden it the day before the grader was due that year!

Warburton is the largest community within the Indigenous Ngaanyatjarra lands, and was a study in contrasts. Chaotic activity around the fuel pumps, where people were filling up everything from beat-up old town cars to the latest fully accessorised four-wheel drives towing enormous caravans, and locals sitting under shady trees watching the world go by without a care. The town cars roared in and out of the roadhouse in a cloud of dust, coming back several minutes later with a new load of occupants. This went on the whole time I was there—it was hectic.

The first order of business was to grab myself a bacon and egg toasted sandwich, which appeared to be the most popular item on offer that morning, and an iced coffee to wash it down. My breakfast table was the ground under the shady trees outside, where I sat down among the locals who were also eating their breakfast sandwiches. It was very relaxing and I enjoyed a bit of social interaction. Plenty of local kids came up to my bike and wanted to sit on it, which I was happy for them to do. I think some of the parents wanted to as well, but I wasn't as keen on that. The kids were a happy bunch, all smiles and laughter as they ran around. It was a pleasure to see.

By the time I'd finished breakfast, it was my turn at the fuel pump. The distance to my next fuel stop was well within the range of my long-range tank alone, but I always liked to carry a healthy reserve supply in case of emergencies, such as an unexpected detour, a track closure or some sort of mishap. I filled up one of my fuel bladders, and so would have a range of over 800 kilometres. That was much more than I would need if everything went to plan, but I couldn't afford to become complacent, even though I'd travelled the next part of the route before. I knew my next fuel stop would be in two days' time at a remote cattle station called Carnegie.

In a cloud of dust, I took off from Warburton, ready for the outback and more solitude.

•

The turnoff for the Heather Highway which runs onto the Gunbarrel Highway is about 40 kilometres west of Warburton on the Great Central Road. The grader gods had smiled on me, as all the way to the turnoff it was a smooth six-lane dirt highway. What a way to cruise along after brekky, I thought. The sun was up, warming me in my riding gear, and the sky was a cloudless blue—life was good. As my friends will tell you, I'm happier riding when the sun's out—it makes me smile. And today I was all smiles.

That didn't last long, though, as when I turned right onto the Heather Highway, I found my old friends the corrugations waiting for me, shaking me wide awake again. I cursed that grader driver for not continuing along my route!

Not far down the Heather Highway was the turnoff to another of Len Beadell's famous roads, the Gunbarrel Highway. The Gunbarrel is an unmaintained track—sections of it have not received any maintenance since its construction in 1958—so you can imagine the shape it was in. Only the wheel tracks of four-wheel drives stopped it from becoming overgrown.

Back in 2018, I'd set off from Canberra to explore the Kimberley region of Western Australia. That trip encompassed crossing east to west across the Tanami Road, and west to east across the Gunbarrel Highway and the Great Central Road. I had covered nearly 11,500 kilometres in a month on my KTM 990 Adventure S. During that trip, I had a stopover in Broome, where Stace flew over to meet me for a short holiday. What a great time we had! The sunsets over Cable Beach were magnificent.

The Kimberley is a wild, rugged area. There's so much natural beauty, with rock formations, waterholes and great camping spots all along the Gibb River Road. During my ride there, I met up with a bloke named Bill, who was travelling on his BMW GS 1200 Adventure, and we ended up travelling most of the Gibb together. Bill, who was from Sydney, was writing a book for charity about his adventures across Australia—and I even got a mention in it.

During our time together, we had camped up at the Windjana Gorge campsite for a couple of days when a man named John pulled up on his BMW GS 1200 and asked if he could camp next to us. We of course said yes, so he kindly offered us a drink. We replied that we had all the water we needed, but he was asking if we wanted a beer! In unison, Bill and I said yes, and that was when I saw one of the most beautiful motorcycling sights I've ever seen.

John went to the back of his bike, which had a big, black-topped box pannier attached, and opened the lid. It was full of ice and cans of beer. He passed us one each and we all sat around having a coldie—it was magnificent.

John told us he was a local road-train driver and had come out from Derby for an overnight camp. What luck, we thought, and we had a great afternoon chatting away and drinking all John's beers.

It was during that 2018 trip that I read a book about Len Beadell and learned about the Gunbarrel Highway and his other exploits. But I hadn't completed anywhere near as much research for that trip as I did for my present ride, so I was caught unaware by the deep sand along the Gunbarrel. Now, when you're on a fully loaded adventure bike without a steering damper, sand is not fun, I can tell you. Even the KTM, with its Dakar heritage, was a handful, as it had to be ridden faster than I was comfortable with to stay on top of the sand. My shoulders were locked solid trying to prevent the handlebars from snapping left and right. It was exhausting, and at the time I hadn't enjoyed it at all.

Uniquely, the KTM carries its battery low down under the motor in front of the bash plate. That lowers the bike's centre of gravity but allows the battery to wiggle around a little in its rubber cradle. In 2018, the constant corrugations of the Gunbarrel were bad enough to snap the positive lead right off the battery, causing the bike to die. Of course, it had to fail when I was in a sandy riverbed. The total loss of electrical power didn't take too long to troubleshoot, but it did take some ingenuity to repair. I had with me a small jump-starter pack, with accompanying leads, one of which I used as a temporary battery cable. With a pair of pliers, cable ties, electrical tape and nuts and bolts, I made a solid repair that lasted all the way home. I'm just glad I didn't get a flat battery on the way. That little setback and a puncture had been the only issues I'd had on the Gunbarrel.

Back in 2018, my first night camping on the Gunbarrel was right next to a rocky outcrop, the only geological formation of any height in what was otherwise a vast, flat, open plain in the Gibson Desert. That afternoon, after setting up camp, I climbed to the top—it must have been 20 to 30 metres high—scrambling up the loose, rocky surface in my old rubber thongs. I'd brought a bottle of rum and a warm can of Coke, which luckily hadn't exploded in my tank bag.

I found a comfy spot with a commanding view across the Gibson Desert, sat down and poured a drink into my metal camp mug. I toasted the solitude and had a sip. This was my first experience of real isolation, and it was like nothing I'd felt before. I hadn't seen a soul all day, I was miles from anybody, I'd just fixed a flat tyre and I was still going. I felt invincible. The only noise was a gentle breeze rustling the nearby mulga trees. There were no birds, just me and the desert—it was bliss. It was like a drug. I loved it and knew I wanted more.

Today, as I skimmed over the sandy section on the DR, bouncing from wheel track to wheel track with ease, I thought about how much my sand riding had improved. In 2018 it was slow going, bogging down, swerving off the track, swearing, sweating and generally having a miserable time. Back then, the sand seemed to go on forever and my heart sank every time I went around a bend and saw more, but this time I couldn't have cared less. Everything was working well. It had taken me the better part of half a day to get through this section on the 990, but the DR650 dispensed with it in a few hours.

Sand—must attack. Speed is your friend & also your enemy. Use wisely.

Sunday, 30 July

The track was familiar to me, but the years had weathered the surface and the scrub was slightly different. Yet the atmosphere was the same. I recognised changes in the landscape, like the dry creek beds, rocky outcrops and texture of the track.

One landmark I was keeping a lookout for was a long straight with a slight incline. As I'd come in the opposite direction in 2018, it had been a decline, but I remembered that the view at the top was spectacular. I'd taken a photo of the 990 here in 2018 and I wanted to find the spot again. As luck would have it, the scenery was familiar enough for me to locate it.

It was with a sense of nostalgia that I lined up the DR in a similar position, but pointing in the opposite direction. I took a couple of pictures and thought about how much better prepared I was this time around: how much lighter and more capable my set-up was, and how much I'd progressed as an outback rider.

After the photoshoot, I ate my lunch, which that day was tuna, lentils and black rice—my favourite—followed by a handful of sugar jubes. I always enjoyed lunchtime—who doesn't like eating, right? Then, having completed my little trip down memory lane, I refocused on the task at hand—setting a Guinness World Record—and rode off again.

The track was now a mixture of hardpack rocks and ironstone gravel and corrugations, nothing I hadn't crossed before, so I managed to keep up a good pace. The kilometres melted away during the next few hours of riding.

As I crested a rise in the ironstone twin track, I saw an older white LandCruiser in the distance. It was pulled off the track and parked under a couple of trees, although I couldn't immediately see anyone around it. I decided I had better pull up, as you do, just to see if everything was okay and have a chat. Apart from the pleasure of meeting other travellers, it's always sensible to seek any information about the track conditions you're heading into, and to be aware of any dangers.

I stopped the bike on the track, not wanting to ride into the scrub for fear of a puncture. It was, after all, a mulga stick that had punctured my KTM the last time I was here, and I wasn't keen to repeat that episode. As soon as I'd turned off the bike, out from underneath the LandCruiser shot a smiling little English staffy, wagging its tail profusely. It ran straight over to me, obviously keen to meet the visitor.

I got off my bike, took off my helmet and gave the staffy a pat—what a wonderfully friendly little doggo he was. While I was making a fuss of this little fella, his owner, Steve, walked over as well and introduced himself.

Steve and his dog, Ned, had travelled from Bunbury, in the south of Western Australia, and were tackling the Gunbarrel from west to east before heading home again. His old LandCruiser was solid as a rock, he reckoned, and he'd encountered no issues with it whatsoever. He told me a few stories of the travellers he'd met along the track, some of them enjoying the solitude and having a great time of it, and others at the end of their tether because of the horrendous corrugations and wanting to get out of there as soon as possible. It wasn't easy going, he said, but wasn't that why we did this sort of thing?

I agreed with him, and we discussed the pros and cons of outback travel. I did wonder to myself, though: *How bad could it be driving the Gunbarrel?* Apart from being slower than a bike, it was a hell of a lot more comfortable. What were those people expecting when they came out here?

Like me, Steve had a passion for the outback and all it had to offer. He said he was off to do the Anne Beadell Highway the following year, and I gave him a few tips on things he should see, with the Emu Field test site being one of them. Before I left, I asked Steve if he'd mind being a witness for my Guinness World Record attempt, and he kindly obliged. I gave Ned one last pat before jumping back on the bike and getting on with my ride.

•

The rest of the afternoon passed uneventfully. I didn't see any more vehicles, so it was just me and the Gibson Desert. I got into a good rhythm with the bike, feeling very comfortable with my speed, so I decided to push on towards the maintained section of the Gunbarrel. This stretched out about 100 kilometres eastward from Carnegie Station, where I would be stopping in tomorrow. I knew from experience that the track would improve a lot, making the ride tomorrow a whole lot easier, so I was looking forward to it. I also knew that there was a campsite with bore water in the area, so I kept a lookout for the unmarked turnoff into the bush, as this would be my overnight stop.

It was nearly sunset when I arrived at the oasis of Geraldton Bore which is on the western boundary of the Gibson Desert. A hand-powered pump provides underground water to the surface, and while it is drinkable, it's hard on the palate. Originally installed in 1982 by the Geraldton Historical Society, and now maintained by four-wheel drive clubs, the bore provides a year-round source of lifesaving water.

I'm always a bit wary of setting up camp in areas that see frequent human use. The dingoes out here are cunning and get to know where the humans are—and where there are humans, there's food scraps to be scavenged. Not that I've ever been attacked or frightened by the dingoes, but more because they're a nuisance and can get into your food supplies if you don't stow them properly. I've seen more dingoes around campsites like this than at any of the stealth camps in the middle of the bush I've set up, so I made a mental note to keep things tidy tonight. My preference would have been to camp away from here, but tonight was shower time!

I set up my tent before it got dark and grabbed my biggest water bladder, which held six litres, and filled it from the hand pump. Now, this water bladder has a handy attachment that screws into the spout, turning it into a small shower head. When twisted, it sprays water out just like a shower—brilliant!

I found a low branch that I could sling the bladder onto and stripped off under it. It felt great to wash all the dust off myself, leaving me feeling clean and fresh—a good way to go to bed tonight.

I'd crossed seven deserts now and made great progress today, with nearly 500 kilometres covered, so I was pleased. I had a few options for tomorrow, as I was well ahead of my planned itinerary, which had me stopping for the night at Carnegie Station. At this rate I would definitely beat my twenty-day estimate.

I decided that I'd sleep on it and see how I felt when I got up.

Very tiring the concentration & track selection. Peaceful now, just made a brew, sun going down, lovely relaxed, feels familiar. Easy run on good road tomorrow. Now two days ahead of planned schedule. Not pushing silly fast, just steady and consistent. Bike running perfectly. Been dreaming about if I get the official record—excited. Don't count your chickens. Not eating as much, brought too much food, couple of spare meals due to pace. Gunbarrel is easy compared to Connie Sue. Don't ever want to see that or Anne Beadell Highway again! I think my desert riding days are over after this. Don't know if I want to put my mind and body through this again.

Sunday, 30 July

On my way to the starting point at Marree, South Australia. The drive up through the Flinders Ranges is spectacular.

And so it begins, leaving Marree on day one of my epic Guinness World Record ride.

When I reached Eyre Creek it was in full flood! The water was rushing and in parts looked over 40 metres wide. I just couldn't see how I'd get across.

The marker post at Poeppel Corner, Simpson Desert where the states of South Australia, Queensland and the Northern Territory meet. All I remember were the flies!

Salt flats near Poeppel Corner, Simpson Desert, South Australia.

The French Line, Simpson Desert, South Australia. Even with all the rain the landscape still looked arid. This is closed in summer due to temperatures exceeding 50 degrees Celsius.

The Pedirka Desert, South Australia, Australia's smallest desert. It's so tiny that I forgot about it and rode right through without realising!

Entering the Great Victoria Desert, one of the most remote regions in the country.

Corrugations for hundreds of kilometres. This was the terrain that worried me the most, as it could easily damage my bike due to the extreme vibrations and constant pounding on the suspension. Ride too slow and I could sink into them and get badly shaken about; ride too fast and I could lose control.

Typical camp for the night and seeing what was for dinner. Variety in my ration packs was essential and I always looked forward to sitting down and having an evening coffee.

Morning in the Great Victoria Desert, feeling good and stopping for a morning snack.

Neale Junction, Great Victoria Desert, Western Australia, hundreds of kilometres from anything.

It was great to meet Andrew and Michelle on the Connie Sue Highway and stop for a chat. *Andrew Kennett*

The gorge about 300 metres from my camp on the Connie Sue Highway, Gibson Desert, Western Australia.

Geraldton Bore,
Gunbarrel Highway,
Western Australia.

The start of the Canning
Stock Route at Wiluna.

13

Deflated

31 July

> *Today woke up sore—neck/shoulders aching, as well as hands and wrists.*
>
> *Monday, 31 July*

I WAS AHEAD OF MY DAILY DISTANCE TARGETS; THIS GAVE ME options to push further than planned. That's what I would do today, see how far I could go, and where I ended up depended on the difficulty of the terrain ahead of me.

The ride from Geraldton Bore to the graded road was about 35 kilometres, and I was sure glad to reach it. The constant pounding had taken a toll and I was feeling it today. The smoother surface gave my aching body a rest from the constant beating it had taken over the previous days. It also allowed my mind to rest, as I didn't have to stay as alert to obstacles and track changes. It gave me time to think about my plan for the day.

It was about 550 kilometres to Wiluna, where I had posted a resupply package to the post office. If I was going to collect it today, I had to be in Wiluna before the post office closed. I'd then need to get out of town, as there was nowhere to stay there. So I might as well push hard to get onto the Canning Stock Route, I figured, making it a day of more than 600 kilometres. Soreness or not, I was here to break a Guinness World Record!

I twisted the throttle on the little DR, unleashing a few more of those angry 40 or so ponies I had underneath me, and picked up the pace. The long day ahead made me thankful for the custom seat I had fitted to my bike. Back when I bought the bike, I ordered a more comfortable seat to be made by a local upholsterer. It was wider and had a dual layer of foam for additional padding specifically for long-distance touring. On top of that I had fitted a black sheepskin cover, which provided a further layer of softness for my butt. It was made for a day just like this and I was glad I had it.

My next stop would be Carnegie Station, and with the graded road being about two lanes wide it allowed me to move along at a decent rate. I was wary though, as the mulga scrub was thick on each side and I'd seen camels here during my last trip. The last thing I wanted was a repeat of what happened on the Anne Beadell Highway—or, worse still, a camel to run out in front of me.

Carnegie, as it's known locally, is a pastoral lease of about 1.25 million acres that runs a large number of beef cattle. To put that into perspective, it's equal in landmass to the Caribbean country of Trinidad and Tobago, which has a population of 1.5 million people. At this time of year Carnegie has a population of less than ten. I'd stopped here in 2018 to refuel and would do so again today.

I made it to Carnegie around midday and was greeted by every available station dog, along with the caretakers Alex and Grace. Both in their twenties and loving the freedom that station life provides, they had been out here for a number of years. This morning they'd been busying themselves with routine upkeep of the place while the station managers were away. They were used to having all sorts of travellers drop into Carnegie as it was the last fuel stop until Warburton to the east or Wiluna to the west.

When I was here in 2018, I'd camped overnight, which had been a great experience. Back then it was mustering time at the station, so there were many station hands around and mustering vehicles of all shapes and sizes parked around the living quarters. It looked like a scene out of *Mad Max*! Some of these vehicles had battle scars from run-ins with scrub bulls, and were covered in dents and in various states of rustiness. I'd spent a memorable evening by the campfire with the mustering crew swapping stories.

Today would be a different day for Alex. He'd seen his fair share of travellers passing through but only one other like me. I didn't realise it at the time, but when I started telling him about my attempt to break a Guinness World Record for the fastest crossing of all ten Australian deserts, he began looking at me with some familiarity. He'd been working at Carnegie when Benji Brundin the current record holder had passed through on his record attempt—what a coincidence! We had a chuckle and chatted about it for a while. To mark the occasion, Grace took a photo of us and they both signed up as witnesses on my behalf.

With my decision to press on made, I didn't stay around very long. I filled up with fuel and got myself organised, then thumbed the starter as the station dogs crowded around me. As soon as I hit the magic button, they all started barking and running around in a cloud of dust, and they chased me out the gate and down the road as fast as they could. I beeped the horn and waved goodbye to Grace and Alex. It had been a pleasure stopping at Carnegie, which is such a hospitable place in the middle of nowhere. I was disappointed to be leaving so soon.

•

It was about four hours' ride to Wiluna, which was comfortably doable as long as I didn't have too many breaks. I still had the lower gearing on but I couldn't be bothered stopping to change the sprockets again, so I just rode as fast as I could without over-revving the motor. It was times like these that I wished for the top speed of the KTM on these long dirt stretches.

> Just kept riding to Wiluna & decided to get on the CSR tonight. Nervous, but it can't be harder than the ABH, can it?
>
> Monday, 31 July

The bike had been running really well—so well, in fact, that I'd forgotten about the earlier issue with the steering. Nothing else had vibrated loose and I hadn't touched a cable tie for a few days now. The thing that worried me the most was the weight of everything I was carrying on the subframe. The DR is designed to carry a pillion passenger on the seat, where the frame is braced and strong. I had a bit more weight over the rear of the seat on the rear rack, where the frame was weaker.

Even though my saddlebags were on the seat, I'd seen images and read stories of subframes cracking down near the foot pegs. That was something I checked every day as part of my routine visual inspection. I'd seen one of those cracked subframes repaired out in the bush with some fencing wire—a rough repair, but it did the job. I had included some light-gauge fencing wire in my tool kit as a result.

I was glad I'd chosen the DR650 for this ride. It was its simplicity that had drawn me to it: an air-cooled motor with no radiator or plumbing to worry about, and only a small oil cooler that was tucked away out of harm's way. The lack of electronics was also a bonus—no sensors to bugger up, no error codes to read, and most importantly no fuel injection and the associated fuel pumps to fail. The DR had an old-school carburettor that was easy to fix in the event of a fuel blockage or a dose of bad fuel. The carburettor could easily be removed and the jets cleaned out—you didn't need any special tools. The current DR was designed in 1996, and it hasn't changed since then. In my opinion it's the most reliable bike for outback travel there is.

Funnily enough, though, it wasn't my first choice of bike. You might recall that originally I was planning to ride the Canning Stock Route (CSR). I'd seen a few ride reports and plenty of four-wheel drive reports, and it seemed like the ultimate challenge. Huge distances between fuel stops, remote areas, big sand dunes—what more could you want? At that time, my only bike was the KTM 990 Adventure S, which I knew was too big and heavy.

I'd been riding with my mate Clancy who had a KTM 690, which was a real rocket ship. It took me back to the old days when I was riding my Honda XR600RM, and it seemed like the right size bike for the job. Its sister bike, the Husky 701, appealed more to me, and it wasn't long before I found one up in Coffs Harbour. I rang the guy who was selling it and said I'd come and have a look at it the next morning. After a long drive up from Canberra, I saw the bike—it was in great shape—and bought it on the spot, trailering it home the same day.

I just couldn't get over the power of this single-cycle machine—it went hard! I was really enjoying the forest riding around Canberra, but it wasn't long before I turned my mind to upgrades for a desert trip. Any bike I took on the CSR had to have a fuel range of at least

900 kilometres, and I set about figuring out how to upgrade the Husky 701. There were a number of options I could try, but as I was working on these a few things started playing up.

First, I couldn't stop the clutch master cycling from leaking. I replaced the cap with a new plastic one but it still leaked. I purchased an OEM Husky billet cap, and it leaked less but still wept fluid. The rear brake master cylinder then also started leaking—it eventually failed and had to be replaced. I took the Husky on a couple of overnight camping trips and found the positioning of the fuel tank and filler cap at the rear of the bike annoying, as I had to unpack my luggage each time I needed to fill up with fuel. The positioning of the muffler also burned a hole in my riding pants due to its excessive heat. I was starting to doubt my purchase.

As part of the upgrading process, I bought a rally tower and fairing kit from a well-known European brand. Upon installation, I discovered the kit was poorly made and didn't fit well, causing components to not align properly, which would place them under stress when tightened. I was concerned that this component would fail from the constant vibration of the CSR's corrugated roads.

After a few months of trying to figure out extra fuel-carrying capacity, I came to the conclusion that this wasn't the bike for long-distance remote desert travel. I wasn't comfortable with the number of modifications I needed to make, and the quality of some of the aftermarket parts was questionable. The bike just didn't give me the confidence I needed if I was going to go where I intended. If I was just riding around the forests of Canberra, I would have kept it, however I decided to move it on.

After the 701 was gone, I called up a well-known Suzuki dealership in New South Wales and ordered a brand-new Suzuki DR650, with all the accessories I needed: the big fuel tank, upgraded suspension, a custom seat and steering damper. Right out of the box this bike would be ready for outback desert travel. I was more used to old-school air-cooled carburettor bikes anyway, like the XRs of previous years, so it was perfect.

My ride with Farmer and Kurtis in 2022 provided the ideal opportunity for me to test all the accessories on the bike. I learned what worked, what didn't and what I needed to improve. After that 2022 trip, increasing the suspension spring rates was the only major modification I made.

I arrived in Wiluna a bit after 4pm, with plenty of time to collect my resupply package. Wiluna has a population of about 600 people, and it's an essential stop for travellers entering and leaving the CSR. It's the only place for fuel and supplies for nearly 1000 kilometres if you're heading onto the CSR. The post office is inside the local IGA supermarket, which is part of the roadhouse and service station and provides travellers and the local community alike with all the supplies they need.

I went to the petrol bowsers first to fill up. I don't even bother looking at the price of fuel in these outback towns—I mean, what's the point if you have no choice? It's not like you won't buy it. Petrol is a necessity, so you just buy what you need. Today I took onboard 58 litres of fuel, which would give me a range of nearly 1000 kilometres, as I was about to embark on the longest leg of my trip without fuel available. My next fuel stop would be the community of Parnngurr approximately 850 kilometres away, and I liked to have that little buffer the additional fuel provided.

My next job was to go into the post office and collect my parcel, hoping that it had arrived in one piece. I'd also forwarded myself a new rear tyre just in case. The rear I had on was only about 30 per cent worn and had no cuts or tears, so I decided that while it might have been nice to have a new tyre, I didn't want to waste time changing it or risk pinching a tube. The sand riding wasn't wearing it out very fast anyway, so I was sure it would last another week with no problems. I collected my food package and arranged to post the tyre home again. All that postage probably made it the most valuable 17-inch rear knobbly tyre in the country!

My food packages consisted of another seven or so ration packs, plus a tube of condensed milk. As I was a couple of days ahead of schedule, I wouldn't need all the new ones I had posted. I packed what I thought I needed and then gave the rest away to some of the locals who were watching what I was up to. They were grateful for the lollies inside, but I'm not sure they were as keen on the dehydrated meals. I managed to squeeze just over a week's worth of food and my full water bladders back into the saddlebags, which were now bursting at the seams. That, plus the additional two full fuel bladders on top, made the bike super heavy, and it was sitting down quite low. It was the heaviest it had been all trip, and made me uneasy about encountering sand. The suspension was doing its job, but the additional weight was definitely noticeable. It felt like a whale of a thing when I sat on it.

While I was pushing and squeezing all this stuff into my bike, a six-wheel drive LandCruiser pulled up. It was one of those remote adventure holiday rigs that could carry a few passengers on a fully catered trip along the CSR. It was fully kitted out with high-lift suspension, big tyres and black windows—it looked tough. While I was giving away my ration packs, I saw the driver coming out of the IGA supermarket with bags full of ice cream cakes and beers to stock up what I assumed were numerous fridges. That was the luxury way to do the CSR!

One of the customers from the tour came over. She was a lady in her mid-fifties and was interested in what I was up to. I told her where I was going and that I was attempting to break a Guinness World Record. She didn't seem very surprised, and promptly told me that there was someone ahead of me on another motorbike doing the same thing, but with two support vehicles. Before I got a chance to ask some questions, she wandered off not knowing the true effect of what she'd just said to me.

What did she mean? Was there someone else on a motorbike just out for a ride along the Canning? Was there someone else on a motorbike attempting to break the same Guinness World Record, but with a support crew? It didn't make sense to me. I was fatigued and a little confused, questioning what I had heard. Did I misinterpret what she just told me? Possibly.

My mind started racing and second guessing what I thought I'd just heard. I didn't know what to believe.

I tried to put it out of my head, and continued to prepare my bike for the next leg of the journey. I had to make sure I had everything I would need, that everything was tied down properly and that there was no damage or maintenance issues on the bike, as I would be far from civilisation for the next week.

Once I was satisfied that I was good to go, I slowly rode out of town, getting used to the heavy, wallowing beast that the DR had become. Thankfully, the road all the way out to the CSR was another wide and graded surface, giving me time to adjust to the different dynamics of the heavier bike.

It was at times like these that the weight over the subframe was at the front of my mind. With both full bladders on the back, there was very little room for me to squeeze in between them and the tank in front. If I stood up, I could basically sit on top of them. It wasn't very comfortable but wouldn't last too long. I was still thinking about what that woman had said. Was there another rider in front of me, and what were they doing?

•

The CSR is the longest stock route in the world at just a touch over 1800 kilometres. Running from Wiluna to Halls Creek, it was used to open up the cattle trade in Western Australia. It was constructed in the early 1900s by Alfred Canning and a team of about 30 men, 70 camels and 100 tonnes of food, including a large number of goats for meat and milk. Fifty-four water sources, including wells, were identified to water the cattle during the arduous journey, with the first drove along the stock route commencing in 1910.

The CSR has been in Australian folklore for decades as the hardest four-wheel driving track in the country. Only a handful of motorcycles have successfully traversed its length unsupported by any vehicle or aircraft. Of the 54 original water sources, there were only a small number left that I could rely on if I ran out of water, so it was a commodity that I had to carefully manage and protect.

I arrived at the turnoff to the CSR and stopped to take a couple of photos. I was super-excited to finally be here. I remembered travelling through Wiluna in 2018 on the KTM and seeing four-wheel drives coming off the CSR wondering what it was like. Well, today

I was about to find out for myself. I had plenty of food, water, fuel, communications gear and tools, so it was a case of now or never.

I rode slowly into the scrub towards Well 2, just soaking in the moment. I was finally here! As I rode along, though, I kept an eye out for motorbike tracks, just in case that lady at the servo had been right.

I started thinking about finding a camp for the night. There was half an hour or so of daylight left and I wanted to get set up before it got too dark. I passed Well 2 and saw a large, flat grassland area surrounded by desert oak trees and thought it looked like a nice spot to spend the night. I steered the DR off the track and across the grassland, pulling up near a couple of the smaller trees, then I turned off the bike. I was about 500 metres off the track.

Instantly I was struck by the silence: there were no birds squawking, no insects buzzing, nothing, just the *tick, tick, tick* of my engine as it slowly cooled down. It was so peaceful, and I was ecstatic just being here, and for making it that far. I just stood there for a moment with my helmet off, looking around and taking it all in. 'I'm on the Canning Stock Route,' I said to myself out loud.

Pretty soon the ringing in my ears had passed and I'd adjusted to my surroundings, so I started making camp. By now I was an old hand and had my tent and sleeping kit up and ready in about twenty minutes.

This was my favourite time of day. I made a brew and sat down just on dusk, sipping on my caramel latte as I sent a few messages home. My Garmin had been pinging like crazy from my support crew, who had been following my progress. Everyone knew it was a big day for me today and so they were all sending messages of support.

I messaged my riding buddies about what the lady at Wiluna had told me. Was she right? Did I have a rival in front of me? I wasn't sure, but the idea of it unnerved me. The guys all messaged back quickly, encouraging me to go hard tomorrow and chase this 'ghost' rider down.

Despite my concerns, my first night on the CSR was a good one. I'd ridden almost 600 kilometres today and had only three more deserts to cross. I was getting close.

> Fuelled up—58 litres heavy—whale. Lady tourist from four-wheel drive tour group came off CSR and said a motorbike rider was ahead of me doing the same thing but with two support vehicles. Annoyed? Unsure? Deflated? Stick to the game plan—see what happens. Good kilometres today. Hopefully two more camps to Parnngurr—reassess then.
>
> Monday, 31 July

14

Concentration

1 August

I WOULD REMAIN ON A NORTHERLY TRACK FOR THE NEXT FIVE DAYS as I traversed the Canning Stock Route. Sometime today I would enter desert number eight, the Little Sandy Desert, and push for as many kilometres as I could.

It was happening: today was the day I'd get to ride the Canning Stock Route. This had been a dream of mine for a very long time, and I felt grateful to be here on the start line.

Information about the CSR—its track conditions, and the distances to travel for fuel and water—had been hard to come by. What information I did find was often contradictory. Most had been from four-wheel drivers, so unfortunately their trip reports were only really relevant to other four-wheel drive vehicles, as they travelled much slower than a motorbike. There were a few motorcycle ride reports and stories I'd managed to find on internet forums that were helpful, but they weren't bike-specific and were out of date: the terrain had changed dramatically since they were written. Even fewer were ride reports from guys who had ridden the CSR unsupported, which would have been the most valuable for me. On this stretch, I'd have to rely more than ever on my own abilities to get me through.

I'd had a very broken sleep, tossing and turning all night. My mind had been churning over this leg of the ride: I couldn't shake thoughts of the extra weight of my bike, laden down with all my extra fuel, water and supplies, and the unknown track conditions ahead from my mind. In the end, I'd had only a few hours' sleep.

However, I maintained my routine. I always enjoyed breakfast just as much as dinner, as it gave me time to plan, and today was no different. I boiled the billy and made coffee with a little extra condensed milk for sweetness. It's funny how you crave things when you can't have them. For me that was a nice milky coffee, and coffee with condensed milk was the next best thing. The remaining hot water went into a little apple and cinnamon porridge sachet, to which I added a little more condensed milk. That was a good breakfast for me. I don't like to start off the day's riding feeling too full, as it makes me feel sluggish. It was just enough energy to get me going.

Today's ride started slowly. The extra 60 kilograms the bike was carrying made it feel like I had a pillion passenger on the back. The DR moved and wobbled around a lot on the uneven surface. Again I hoped I wouldn't encounter any deep sand—I didn't need a fall this early. I also didn't want to bend the subframe by charging too hard, so it was a balancing act for a while. I kept telling myself that this was a marathon, not a sprint.

Once the kilometres started adding up, I could start removing some of the weight off the back of the bike by emptying the fuel bladders into my main tank. Given that the DR was using between five and six litres per 100 kilometres, I calculated, it would take me about 200 kilometres to use a full 12-litre fuel bladder.

The southern end of the CSR is the rocky part, and today I crossed over hundreds of kilometres of sharp rocks and stones as the track wove around the hills and gullies of the Frere Range. It was real puncture country. There were only two wheel tracks for me to follow, and I stuck in them religiously, figuring that the rocks in the wheel tracks were worn and smooth, not sharp like the rocks outside them. That was my theory, anyway, and it worked, as I didn't get any punctures. In and out of the rock gardens were patches of hardpack clay, which opened up like small claypans, allowing me to pick up the speed occasionally.

The countryside along the majority of the CSR is low-lying spinifex grassland. This stuff seems to grow as well among the rocks as it does in the sand country, so any off-track excursion should not be taken lightly for fear of punctures. Spinifex grass has sharp spines that love to puncture motorcycle tyres and generally stick into anything else they can find, such as oil coolers. They're a real nuisance.

The temperature out here was noticeably higher than I'd experienced before. By midday it was approaching 30 degrees and was getting uncomfortable. I had ditched my riding jacket a couple of days previously, stowing it in the duffel bag on the back of the seat, and was only riding with a jersey and armour underneath.

For this trip, I'd purchased all new riding gear. I wanted waterproof gear this time, as when Farmer and I did our desert trip in 2022 I'd had to stop a number of times to put on and take off a rainsuit, which was a real pain—plus that was additional riding gear that had to be carried even if not used. I'd purchased some new lightweight Gore-Tex riding pants and jacket, which negated the need for outer rainwear.

This lightweight Gore-Tex gear was top-notch, very comfy and with a decent amount of venting, but it certainly wasn't summertime stuff. I'd opened all the vents in my pants, and with the mesh jersey and armour underneath, that allowed as much airflow onto my body as possible. But after about 10am the airflow just got hotter and hotter—it was a bit like standing in front of a hairdryer. But riding with any less protection would have been dangerous.

I'd filled my three-litre CamelBak to the brim today, hoping to stave off the dehydration I'd suffered when crossing the Simpson. As the temperature increases, water becomes your most vital resource, and it's only when you're consuming a lot that you realise just how important it is to carry enough. If I had no mishaps, I was confident that I had a sufficient supply to get me through to Parnngurr.

The landscape of the red ironstone rocks and hills was a stark contrast to what I'd thought the CSR would be like. As the track was meandering around the rocky outcrops, a number of small freshwater lakes became visible, and I wondered how often they filled up. There had been a lot of recent rainfall, which had obviously filled them this time, but that was no doubt unusual. Most of the time, I thought, they would have just been large claypans. The sight of these bodies of water was spectacular: it was a lot different from what I'd seen back in the sand country.

While riding along and scanning the track in front, I'd occasionally get a glimpse of a motorbike tyre track in the softer ground. I couldn't believe it! Was that woman telling the truth? How old were these tracks? Did I have a competitor? What sort of bike was it? I didn't know. I also looked for recent four-wheel drive tracks to see if it might have been a supported rider. I had a lot of unanswered questions, but I had no choice but to keep on riding, mulling them over in my mind. Maybe there would be a visitors' book up ahead at one of the wells that would give me a clue.

•

The highlight of my day was arriving at Well 6, Pierre Springs—named after Alfred Canning's second Aboriginal guide, Tommy Pierre. This cool little retreat is a real oasis in the desert, with its shady gum and acacia trees providing a thick canopy that blocks the beating sunlight. The well here is one of a few that have been fully refurbished along the route, but the quality of the water was unknown so I didn't risk drinking any.

All the refurbished wells have big metal doors on top to stop wildlife from getting in. It's not unusual for smaller animals like snakes to go into a well and get trapped, along with bigger ones like camels, which can break through and fall in. When that happens, the dead animals pollute the water and make it unusable for everyone, so the metal trapdoor must stay shut.

There was a basic hand winch over the well attached to a large metal pail. It was around midday when I arrived, and I was really feeling the heat, so I took the opportunity to refresh by splashing some cool water on my face. I didn't fill up any of my water bladders, as I was confident I had enough for the next two days.

For emergency situations I carried a small water filtration system that would filter out all the solids, bacteria and parasites, some water purification tablets that would take care of any pathogens, and a billy to kill the rest. I was confident that if I had to use a dubious water source in a survival situation, I could safely produce drinking-quality water for myself.

I had a bite to eat and checked the visitors' book. Some bloke was boasting how good his big American ute was … then another entry caught my eye. The day before, two small trucks had passed through heading north, and in their party was a dirt bike. Aha! There was no mention of any record attempt, though:

it was clearly just a motorcyclist and his mates out for a ride and a drive.

Any record attempt had to be unsupported, so this confirmed for me that there was no one in front of me challenging the record. It was indeed the previous day's fatigue that had caused the confusion, casting doubt in my mind, and I was now glad to be rid of it. These guys must have passed that organised tour group I saw in Wiluna, so I was confident that they were the source of that lady's story. I sighed as relief flooded over me and I had a little chuckle. The odds of a competitor just one day ahead of me was as remote as I was. I should have known better. Anyway, that was the good news story for the day.

I took the opportunity while I was stopped in the shade to transfer more fuel from a fuel bladder into the main tank. I'd covered enough ground this morning to drain one bladder entirely, which immediately changed the handling of the bike. It took about ten kilograms of weight off the rear, reducing the stress on the subframe. Now I could worry less about the bike's frame and have an easier ride in the afternoon.

•

After a fifteen-minute break, I set off again in the midday heat and immediately noticed a bit more sand on the track. I saw my first vehicle for the day around 2.30pm, a couple of travellers in their four-wheel drive heading south. I stopped and met David and Raylene from Chinchilla, Queensland.

David was a bike rider like me, and wouldn't you know it, also owned a DR650. That made him the third guy I'd met on this trip who owned one! Needless to say, he was interested in looking over my bike and talking about the modifications. It was nice to meet another rider who understood how tough what I was doing was. Before I left, David happily witnessed my passage through the Little Sandy Desert.

I wanted to keep pushing on, as the afternoons, like the mornings, were a good time to ride because it was cooler. Up ahead I could see grey clouds forming, and I wondered whether they would bring any rain. It was only a month or two previously that the CSR had been flooded, receiving a significant amount of rainfall. This had closed all the tracks, stopping all travellers entering and stranding those who were already on the route. Rain in outback desert country has a dramatic effect on your ability to ride or drive on the tracks. Sometimes the only thing you can do is take a pause and wait for the tracks to dry out—another reason it was imperative to pack more than enough food and water.

By late afternoon I was back into the sand country again, twin corrugated wheel tracks weaving up and around sand ridges. I was used to it now but it was hard work. There was never a straight section, making it hard to keep up my momentum. For kilometre after kilometre this continued, and I could feel the energy sapping out of me as I wrangled the heavy bike. My wrists and hands were copping the brunt of it, going numb after about one hour of riding now. I tried gripping the handlebars differently, removing one hand at a time when I could and stretching them to no avail. My right hand and wrist was the worst as it was my throttle hand and couldn't be removed from the handlebars as much as the left. It was the constant vibration from the corrugations going up into the handlebars that caused it. It had been getting progressively worse since I left Coober Pedy on the Anne Beadell Highway, and was now a factor in how long I could continuously ride for in between rest breaks.

I was finding it harder and harder to stay focused, and had to keep refocusing my view. I started seeing weird shapes in the landscapes around me, which was another sure sign of fatigue. I was aware of this but had to push through. 'Stay hard,' I kept repeating.

I'd read many stories and reports about how the sand takes on a different texture at different times of day. I didn't think this was possible, or that—if it was—it wouldn't really make much difference. Now I was experiencing the effect first-hand, and it did change things a lot. In the morning, when the overnight temperatures had cooled the sand, it was quite firm and easier to ride on. As the temperatures rose throughout the day, peaking in the early afternoon, the sand loosened up and was more difficult. The bike would sink in deeper if you didn't keep your speed up. Much to my surprise, the effect was really noticeable. Now, as evening approached and the air cooled, I could take advantage of the firmer sand beneath me.

About an hour before I stopped for the day, rain started sprinkling down—what a relief! It was instantly cooling and compacted the sand, which made riding a whole lot easier. That's got to be karma, right? I really needed some relief from the heat and tiredness I was experiencing, and there it was. It was only a light sprinkle, and as long as it didn't get any heavier, I was happy. The country was still dry and it would have to rain a whole lot more before I started to get worried.

As I was riding through the sand ridges, I started looking for a camping spot for the night. I just needed a little clearing in among the ridges. I started making a few exploratory rides off into the spinifex, looking for a flat and open space for my tent. It wasn't long before I found a suitable location and pulled over. I was about 200 metres off the track, but I might as well have been two kilometres away, because the track couldn't be seen at all. It would be so easy to get lost out here if you were disoriented or suffering dehydration and wandered off in the wrong direction. But right now I loved the fact that I couldn't see the track—it added to my sense of isolation and remoteness.

It was still sprinkling rain on and off when I stopped, and I enjoyed the cool change. I was really tired and wanted to set up my camp quickly so I could sit down and have a coffee. Without even thinking, I got everything organised and soon had the billy boiling.

It had been a tough first day on the Canning. All the stories had been right—this truly was rugged country, with long distances of nothingness. It hadn't disappointed so far. I had originally planned to be on it for a week or so, but I'd been making up quite a bit of time. I didn't know what lay ahead or whether I'd make up more time in this section of the ride, but I wasn't going to change my routine now. I had a good rhythm and couldn't afford to fall or to break anything out here, as I was isolated and hadn't been here before. Even so, it was an exhilarating feeling to be out here doing what I loved most.

My Garmin had been beeping for most of the afternoon, so I knew I had plenty of messages to get through tonight. My cheer squad had been in overdrive since learning about a potential challenger. I updated them on the latest information I'd found out about the bike rider and his support vehicles.

I exchanged a number of messages with Stace as I would each night. Every day I would check in to tell her when I started riding and when I had finished. That way she would know I was okay, and tonight was no different.

I was now in desert number eight, the Little Sandy Desert, and had travelled nearly 300 kilometres for the day. The end was in sight—but I had a lot of tough riding to do tomorrow.

> Crap sleep—nervous re CSR. Heavy bike, unknown track. Nurse bike, heavy, rocks & gullies & sand. Transfer fuel when I can. Started rocky & turned to sandy trails. Yes corrugations, but not as bad as the ABH.
>
> Wrist & hand pain all day. Numbness in right hand. Fatigue setting in early arvo. Trees look like kangaroos & big rocks look like cars. Must keep concentrating.
>
> Mechanical sympathy at front of mind, made good kms today, around 300. Camped in sand dunes, so straight into it tomorrow. Bike lighter, though, with bladders getting empty. Keep saying the CSR is just ABH x 2. You can do it!
>
> Cottage pie and mash tonight, yummo. Carrying too much food, travelling further than planned, have more spare rations. Hopefully one more camp, then Parnngurr next day for refuel. Have to push hard in sand tomorrow.
>
> Tuesday, 1 August

15

Get It Done

2 August

Georgia Bore, situated on the northern edge of the Little Sandy Desert was my destination for today. I thought that was achievable, again dependent on track conditions, and it provided drinking water, which was a bonus, making for a good campsite.

All night I heard the pitter-patter of raindrops on my tent fly. Not enough to be concerned about, I noted, but hopefully enough to firm up the sand ahead. I was squarely back in dune country, and they were large. The challenge would be relentless all day.

When I packed up this morning everything was wet. The sand was sticking to everything that touched it, which made for a bit of a mess. That annoyed me. There were some scattered clouds with a few sprinkles of rain, but I didn't mind: the temperature was down. I was keen to make the most of the good conditions. I scoffed down my breakfast and hit the dunes.

> *The rain last night was good, Mother Nature was looking after me to make it easier.*
>
> *Wednesday, 2 August*

My first stop for the day was a famous one for travellers familiar with the Canning Stock Route: Murray Rankin's Trolley. Murray Rankin, a New Zealander, was one of the first people, together with two Englishmen, brothers John and Peter Waterfall, to attempt to walk the entire CSR. In 1972 they set off from Wiluna, pulling behind them homemade trolleys made from lightweight metal tubing and bicycle wheels. Unfortunately, the 1972 attempt was unsuccessful, with Murray having to leave his broken trolley where it still is today, about 20 kilometres north of Well 15, or around 500 kilometres from Wiluna.

Murray tried to walk the CSR in 1973, again unsuccessfully, and it wasn't until 1976 that he succeeded on his third attempt. He was 32 years old when he finally completed the entire journey in just under three months.

What an adventurer! It put a new perspective on endurance and mental toughness. It was quite humbling just standing next to the trolley, thinking about what these men had done. I could just hit my starter button, sit down and ride away. It made my efforts look kind of soft by comparison.

The trolley itself was light and ingenious in its design. It was made of tubing of different diameters that slid inside itself like a sleeve, making the whole thing adjustable in length and width. The sleeves were held in place with grub screws, making the trolley adjustable to suit any track width. The whole thing rolled on two large bicycle rims. Alas, the trolley was now a bit bent out of shape, and the tyres were long gone, but most of the contraption was still there. I was curious to know what improvements Murray made for his second and third versions.

My destination of Georgia Bore was some 300 kilometres through the spinifex and sand country, so it would be another long day in the saddle. Since I was pushing hard, I'd miss out on visiting Durba Springs, another little oasis in the desert. It was the next point of interest on the CSR heading north that I'd encounter, and was only a short deviation off the main track. Yet even that was a deviation I wasn't prepared to risk, not only in terms of lost time, but also in case of an accident. I wouldn't be able to forgive myself if I fell off or broke down while sightseeing off the main route and wasn't able to go on. I'd put too much into getting here to throw it away on a frivolous side excursion.

I will admit, though, being that close and not having a look was disappointing, especially as I'd dreamed about this place over the years because I loved listening to Slim Dusty's song 'End of the Canning Stock Route'. In my mind, Durba Springs was a beautiful place to visit and camp, not dissimilar to Pierre Springs. *Maybe another time*, I thought as I rode past the turnoff.

Over the years, I've ridden across much of the length and breadth of this great country of ours, making multi-week trips at least once a year to the more remote and interesting places. As I mentioned earlier during these trips I'm able to forget about responsibilities at home, issues at work and the current affairs of the day and this is due to the wonderful support of Stace and my family. Stace is used to me being away, taking it all in her stride. Before I bought the Garmin inReach for this trip, she'd been used to not being able to contact me for days at a time and not knowing where I was. Some folks might say this is the perfect arrangement! I knew she trusted my ability to look after myself wherever I was, and she knew I had complete faith in her to look after everything at home while I was away.

Having her rock-solid support makes it so much easier for me on a challenge like this, as it keeps me focused on the task at hand with no distractions. I get into a mindset where I'm thinking of the road ahead—nothing else matters. *Look after the bike, look after yourself, no distracting thoughts, focus on the ride and push yourself.* Day after day after day—it's awesome!

In between the dunes, the countryside varied. Sometimes there was a sandy, corrugated twin track closely lined with slappy sticks, but other times I'd pop out of a densely vegetated area and into a clearing where I could get a real feel for the vastness of the country around me. The years when the track was closed due to the Covid-19 pandemic had caused parts of the track to become badly overgrown, to the point where there were regular broken branches alongside the track, which slowed me down to first gear at times. The regrowth from the gum trees and mulga trees was relentless: at times it was like pushing through a jungle. I was grateful that the four-wheel drives had cleared some of the path, but I wished they'd made it just a bit wider for my handlebars.

When I did get a chance to see the more open country, I looked out at a number of rock formations, small hills and little plateaus. This seemed very unusual here in the middle of nowhere, but because there was nothing else to see, I'd have to stop just to take it in.

I hadn't seen another traveller today, although I was still following the motorbike wheel tracks from the previous day. I wondered how they were getting on with the terrain. *A lot better than me*, I thought, as they had a lighter bike and no luggage, which would have made things a whole lot easier. I also noticed a skinny tyre track every now and again. It looked to be the size of a bicycle wheel but I wasn't sure. I'd seen a lot of crazy cyclists over the years, but on the Canning?

•

As I kept heading north, I was approaching one of the largest salt lakes along the CSR: Lake Disappointment, or Kumpupintil Lake, as it is known by the local Martu people. Lake Disappointment was so named in 1896 by explorer Frank Hann, who was following creeks in the area in search of fresh water. He was unsuccessful, instead locating this large body of salt water, and the name he gave it sums up his feelings at the time. This lake, when full, is about the size of six Sydney Harbours, but not even the recent heavy rainfalls had been enough to fill it.

The scenery changed as I started riding alongside the vast lake: the thick scrub opened right up, with only a scattering of oak trees and lower-lying bushes. The wide view of the beautiful country was magnificent. The sandy ground gave way to a firmer clay base as I skirted the northern edge of the lake bed, which afforded welcome relief to my tired arms. It wasn't until I made it to the crossing at Savoury Creek that I caught a glimpse of the water, though, as there are no real high points from which to view the lake.

Cruising alongside Lake Disappointment was bliss. I'd seen some videos online about the crossing at Savoury Creek and it didn't seem overly problematic, so I wasn't worried about getting across. The only thing that is of concern to dirt bike riders is the depth of water during creek crossings. Everything else can be worked out, just like it did before at Eyre Creek.

As I came around a bend, I saw a small body of water in front of me and thought that must have been the Savoury Creek crossing. I stopped and looked at the GPS display, which confirmed it was Savoury Creek, so I got off to have a look. The crossing didn't look anything like the one at Eyre Creek—it was tiny by comparison, only about ten metres wide. But it pays to be cautious out here, and I wanted to walk across it and determine the firmness of the ground and the depth.

Too many times I've seen people on both bikes and in four-wheel drives go charging into what appears to be a shallow crossing, only to become stuck in deep water or mud. All because they couldn't be bothered getting off their bike or out of their car to have a look. I savoured the chance to hop off and stretch my legs, so I wasn't going to make the same mistake. There was nobody around, and I hadn't seen anyone all day, so there were no fresh wheel tracks going into the creek crossing that I could take as a guide to a safe crossing point. I would have to determine for myself how deep the water was, and how soft the base would be when I rode through.

It was still midafternoon and very hot, and the water looked so appealing that I just wanted to jump in for a swim. As I got to the water's edge I stuck my hand in and tasted the water, as you do. It was super-concentrated salty water—this wasn't what you might call brackish, but saltier than the ocean—bloody horrible! There was no way I was jumping into that. The ground leading up to and into the water was solid, so I didn't think it would present any problems crossing. I grabbed a stick and probed the depth and discovered that wouldn't be a problem either. The only thing I didn't like was that I'd have to ride through water that salty, as it would start corroding parts of my bike.

As part of my preparation before the 2022 desert ride with Farmer and Kurtis, the family and I had gone up to Stockton Beach, in Newcastle, so I could practise my sand riding. I hadn't ridden much sand before and Stockton was the closest large sandy beach area that permitted vehicles to ride and drive on it. You could lap up and down on the firmer sand of the beach area, but there was also a dune area with softer stuff. I'd spent a few days there honing my skills and fine-tuning the DR's set-up for the trip ahead.

I now knew, though, that beach sand is vastly different from sand in the desert. Beach sand is coarser and heavier to ride through: you sink more in beach sand and it saps more power from the bike. Desert sand, in contrast, is firmer and easier to ride in, as it's drier and finer. That's been my experience, anyway.

But my practice at Stockton Beach had taken a toll on the DR. All the salt water and salty air caused corrosion to start attacking all the metal parts straightaway. The chain and sprockets started rusting, the rims started losing their shine, and every scratch on the frame instantly rusted over. So, after each day's practice at the beach I'd take the bike back to where I was staying and hose it down with copious amounts of fresh water to get all the salt off. Even that didn't stop all the corrosion, but it helped.

Practising at Stockton gave me my first introduction to steering dampers and how effective they are in stopping the front from moving around. I experimented with different adjustments, from next to nothing to very stiff, to get some baseline settings that I liked. I was sold on them after that. The whole experience really increased my confidence in sand and taught me how to attack it better. All in all, the trip to Stockton was not only a good family holiday but I left a better rider for it.

Looking at Savoury Creek instantly reminded me of the corrosion at Stockton, but out here I had no hose to wash down the bike at the end of the day. I would have to take it slow through the crossing so as not to splash too much water over the bike—but not too slowly, in case the ground in the middle was soft.

I jumped on the bike and it fired up straightaway. It still amazed me, after all the punishment it had endured, that it was so reliable. It was testament to the DR650's old-school technology. I rode towards Savoury Creek in first gear, slowly wading into the water, which was barely axle-deep, and making my way through. I concentrated on splashing as little as I could onto the bike itself, and before I knew it I had crossed with no problems at all.

•

Soon I was back on the clay surface and following the northern edge of Lake Disappointment. This was good riding, nice and easy, with beautiful scenery to look at, but eventually it steered me back into the sandpit. Then I was back on the foot pegs, gripping the side of the bike as I moved onto another corrugated track.

When riding this terrain, I always stand up and let the bike move around under me. This is a technique you must practise and become accustomed to. My legs are slightly bent and act as shock absorbers to complement the work the suspension is doing. It's like standing in the attack position on a motocross bike: knees bent, arms bent and weight centring over the middle of the bike. For hours on end, though, it's very tiring.

When the sandy, corrugated tracks opened up from twin wheel tracks into a wider road, I could blast along. If there was no vegetation, I would speed up and hit about 80 kph, skipping over the top of the corrugations, allowing the bike to dance around on the sand. Doing this for hour after hour, dramatically increased my sand riding skills.

I started looking for more open sections so I could really open the throttle. Every now and again I'd look at the speedo and realise how fast I was going and back it off a little. It wasn't that it would make much difference to fall off at 80 kph or something more; it was more about how much ability I had in reserve in case something happened. I reckoned I was comfortable at 80 but, in those conditions, not more. Still, it pleased me as I'd become a better rider for it.

It was brutal on the bike, though—I was aware of that. The forks and shock were soaking up enormous amounts of punishment. At this speed, absolutely everything on the bike was shaking badly. The vibrations through the handlebars were horrendous and continued to make my hands go numb. Pretty soon my wrists followed suit and began aching badly. It became very hard for me to continue holding the handlebars with any force for long periods of time. The GPS was shaking all over the place, and I wondered how long it would continue to function in these conditions.

I continued to stand on the pegs, trying to insulate myself from the worst of it and to make it easier on my precious DR. I could put up with a little discomfort, and I would if it ensured my bike stayed in one piece.

A lot of the reports I'd read about the CSR talked about the beauty of the desert scenery and the different terrains you encountered. But I saw little of that. I kept my focus on the road ahead, and only the road ahead. I wasn't here for sightseeing, although I wished I had more freedom to look around and appreciate the country I was riding through. But I was on a mission that didn't afford me that luxury.

It's funny how narrow your focus becomes as the track gets rougher. I was constantly scanning the surface and the edges of the track ahead, so I just didn't have time to look at anything else. If you lift your head and start looking around, you're risking a crash for sure. To really appreciate the remoteness and beauty of the Canning, it has to be travelled at a much slower pace. If I wanted to look at anything, I would stop—it was the only safe way.

•

There was about two hours of daylight left, which gave me enough time to make Georgia Bore—as long as my numb hands and aching shoulders could get me there. I pushed on and kept up a steady pace, though not too fast. I was well aware that in the afternoons, when I was getting tired, I became more prone to making an error and potentially having a crash. So it was about keeping up a steady pace for as long as I could.

At about 6.30pm I rolled into Georgia Bore and couldn't have been happier. I had about 30 minutes of daylight left to set up camp, so there was no time for stuffing around. I turned the bike off and got stuck into it. I knew I'd have time to relax later—and there was nothing worse than setting up camp in the dark.

I can be a very disciplined person when there's work to be done—I just jump straight into it regardless of the situation. Before dark my tent was set up and I was unpacking the rest of my bike.

Georgia Bore, as the name suggests, is another underground water source with a hand pump to bring the bore water to the surface. Unlike Geraldton Bore on the Gunbarrel Highway, though, this underground water supply is drinkable, if a bit hard, and allows travellers to replenish their supplies. It also meant I could have a shower!

Because of the water supply, Georgia Bore was a popular camping spot for four-wheel drivers. Not long after I'd set up, a nearby camper wandered over. I met Chris first, then his wife, Claudia, came over a short time later. Amazingly, Chris and Claudia had both lived in Canberra before, with Chris working at a well-known car repair shop and Claudia at the old Canberra Hospital, which had been demolished in the 1990s. They both now lived in Rockhampton, in central Queensland. We had a quick chat, but I really wanted a shower before it got dark. Chris kindly witnessed my presence in the Little Sandy Desert.

I changed into my Parramatta footy shorts and grabbed the empty six-litre water bladder. I headed over to the hand pump at the bore site and filled it to the brim. At this time there was only Chris, Claudia and me at the campsite, and they were at the southern end, so I took a walk into the bush on my northern end, which also happened to be the other entry and exit point towards Parnngurr community. I walked about 30 metres or so, looking for a tree with a branch at the right height to hang up my water bladder. It's surprising how hard that is when you actually need one!

Eventually I found one and it was shower time. I had brought with me a small toiletry kit with a bit of shampoo and a small microfibre towel, so I was all set. I stripped off, got the water flowing and got under—it was heavenly!

I was getting a good lather up with the shampoo, only to see a convoy of four-wheel drivers entering the campground. I thought about stopping for about a second, then decided no—I was having such a good time, so bugger it! I just turned around and decided they would have to look at my bare arse under the tree all covered in suds! I'm sure there were a few laughs as the vehicles passed. I kept scrubbing and washing and rinsing. The six litres lasted a surprisingly long time, enough for me to get all the dust and grime off myself, and what a relief it was.

I walked back to my tent feeling like a new man. I'd ridden about 275 kilometres today, through some really tough sand county. But all my aches and pains had gone away, and I felt surprisingly normal and ready for tea.

> Started raining last night, was a bit concerned, didn't know how much or how long. Wet pack-up more sprinkles—nervous. Took off wanting to make Georgia Bore, unsure whether doable. Again, Mother Nature looking after me & I rode through energy-sapping dunes, she made it cloudy & had a cool breeze & occasional rain sprinkle. I believe in karma & I reckon today someone paid me back. Very tough riding. Twisty sand, slappy sticks, wrists & hands are very, very sore. Pushed hard, got to Georgia Bore & used my bladder for a shower. Met Chris and Claudia from Rocky. So, all in all, pleased to be here but want to get it done!
>
> Wednesday, 2 August

16

Stay Hard

3 August

I WOULD MAKE A SMALL DETOUR OFF THE CANNING STOCK ROUTE today to refuel, before re-joining and continuing northwards. I had no set campsite identified; I would just ride as far as I could.

During breakfast this morning, I looked over the map. I could tell from the shape of the topographical markings that there would be heavy sand dune country for at least the next two days as I headed north on the CSR. The sand ridge markings on the map were close together nearly all the way to Billiluna, meaning it was hardcore desert riding, and that meant some tough times. I hoped my sore hands and wrists would get me through.

I'd already conquered the French Line, the Anne Beadell Highway and the Gunbarrel, but the CSR was a different beast. It has a way of wearing you down, due not only to the difficult terrain but to its sheer distance—it never seems to end. That plays mind games with you, as well as testing your physical endurance. I tried to stay upbeat. *You've come this far*, I told myself, *you can do it!*

Before I continued north, I needed to detour to the Aboriginal community of Parnngurr, also known as Cotton Creek, to refuel. It was about 80 kilometres off the CSR heading west along the Talawana Track. I hadn't been able to find out much information about the condition of the track, but what I had found had told me it was in reasonable shape. It appeared to be a well-used road, running east–west all the way from the Gary Highway to the mining town of Newman, so I was hopeful of an easy ride into Parnngurr.

I packed up as usual and headed out of Georgia Bore, feeling refreshed and keen for more adventure. Not knowing what lies ahead, day after day, is exciting—new terrain, new scenery and new folks to meet. I loved it!

I followed the four-wheel drive tracks out of the campsite and turned left off the CSR. The road was in pretty good shape: firm, some small rocks and mild corrugations. *If it stays like this*, I thought, *then this will be a good run.*

It didn't! After about 15 kilometres the road turned sandy and extremely corrugated again. I could no longer relax and had to increase my speed to float over the corrugations, while the bike skipped left and right in the foot deep sand ruts that crisscrossed the road.

The four-wheel drives make a real mess of these kinds of roads as they zigzag across the width of the road searching for the smoothest lines, leaving deep ruts running all over the place. The bike has to ride over the top of the sand ruts without losing its front end. That was where my steering damper and speed came into play. I had the damper wound up to about three-quarters from full damping, and had to ride the deep sand between 60 and 80 kph to float over the top of everything. So I was back on the pegs as the bike danced around under me—what a way to wake up!

This sort of riding lasted for about 65 kilometres before the road firmed up again. This allowed me to have a bit more of a look around—and I wanted to stop anyway to give my aching hands a rest. The scenery was desolate—open country with the occasional rocky outcrop—but it looked amazing nonetheless. From then on it was a relatively easy ride into Parnngurr.

One of the things I never do enough is to stop and take pictures. Especially when the going gets tough. The harder it is, the more reluctant I am to stop to take a few photos—I just want to push through. This was even more so during this ride. I had set myself a timetable, so that was always first and foremost in my mind. It's unfortunate to some extent, as the hard stuff is the most interesting … Oh well! I'll have to try harder next time.

Parnngurr has a population of about 150 people, and has basic supplies of food and fuel available for travellers passing through. I had decided to stop rather than risk running out of fuel trying to make it to Kunawarritji, the next community along the CSR.

Without stopping in at Parnngurr, I would have been covering a distance of nearly 1000 kilometres without refuelling. I theoretically had the range, but not with enough margin for error for my comfort. If the sand was deep and I used more fuel than I'd anticipated, I might run out—and that, obviously, would have been a disaster. It was far better to be cautious in these circumstances.

I got into Parnngurr at about 10.30am to see a number of locals milling around the community store and the fuel bowsers. Most vehicles were lined up near the diesel bowser, so I was at the front of the line for Opal. This time I was only going to fill up my main tank. It was about 350 kilometres to Kunawarritji, and a full main tank would give me a range of 600 kilometres, which would be plenty. There was hard riding ahead, too, and I didn't want to make the bike unnecessarily heavy.

The fuel bowsers and general store were on the edge of town, with the school in the middle and all the residential houses scattered around the outskirts. The only green grass I could see were the lawns of the school, a stark contrast with the red dirt roads throughout the rest of the town. The road names seemed easy to remember: First Street, Second Street, Third Street, Fourth Street and Fifth Street—then a jump straight to Tenth Street. Odd! The usual town dogs were out in force, roaming around sniffing and peeing on everything, as they do. Parnngurr seemed like a peaceful place: the pace was slow, no one was in a hurry and life seemed pretty chill. Such a contradiction to my current situation.

After filling up, I headed inside to pay for the fuel. Local stores like this are quite interesting, with a decent variety of canned food and drinks. There was also a decent range of frozen foods for the locals and those travellers lucky enough to have a freezer, but that wasn't me! I bought some water bottles to top up my water bladders, and didn't miss the opportunity to down an iced coffee as well. After all that was done, I turned around and headed out of town again.

I knew what the next 80 kilometres had in store for me, so I put my head down and rode hard, not stopping until I got back to the CSR. My hands and wrists were again aching badly from the vibration of the corrugations, so I took a break at Georgia Bore before turning northwards. My aim for the day was to get as close as I could to Kunawarritji.

•

As I turned north off the Talawana Track, the fun began. Deep, soft sand and a twisty track that kept my speed down. This was difficult—bloody difficult. It was very physical riding and I was soon breathing heavily and sweating heaps. As a consequence, my water consumption rose dramatically and I found myself sucking on the CamelBak drinking tube more and more.

It took all my strength to navigate this section. At times I was down to first gear, unable to gain speed due to the twisty track, and dog-paddling the bike with my feet on the ground either side for stability. This was not fun and my body was aching all over. It was times like this that my mental strength training came to the fore. Over and over, I said to myself, *Stay hard*, as I pushed myself to my limits.

My front wheel was constantly bogging down in the sand as I was going so slowly. All I wanted to do was go faster but the track wouldn't let me. The temperature had risen now and the sand was dry and fine: Mother Nature was really working against me. I was swearing and cursing in my helmet and generally having a tough time of it.

A bit further on was where the dune country that I'd seen on the map started. All the run-ups to the dunes were at right angles, so I couldn't carry much speed, and the deep, sandy tracks twisted all over the place. This was really physical riding. I was trying to ride the DR650 like a lighter motocross bike, carrying as much speed as I could into a corner, then trying to use it as a berm to slingshot myself up the face of the dunes.

The four-wheel drive vehicles as they turned would push the sand to the outside of the corner forming a large mound all the way around. This mound or berm could be used to help steer my bike around the corner. I would approach the corner standing up placing the front wheel into the berm before sitting down, leaning the bike into the corner and twisting the throttle hard to power around the corner to maintain as much momentum as possible to get me up and over the sand dune. Sometimes it wasn't pretty, but it worked!

When it did it was relatively easy going, but occasionally it didn't and I was back to dog paddling like a lunatic, red-lining the motor in first gear and trying desperately not to lose momentum and end up bogged. I was feeling it today.

By lunchtime the temperature had again risen to nearly 30 degrees Celsius and I was exhausted after working so hard. I stopped in a shady spot and nearly fell off my bike as I was getting off, I was so fatigued. I had to strip off some of my riding gear to cool my overheating body, so it was off with my riding pants, jersey and armour to get whatever breeze I could onto myself.

I propped myself up against a tree, still puffing and panting. I was worried about dehydration as I had been sweating profusely all morning. I couldn't drink enough water, and even then I felt like it wasn't really quenching my thirst. Even with the addition of electrolyte tablets to my CamelBak, I still couldn't drink enough.

I sat there for five whole minutes and did nothing until my breathing relaxed and my body cooled. Then I topped up my CamelBak, noting that I'd already drunk nearly two litres today—the most I'd drunk in half a day during the entire ride. I had a decent supply of water to get me through, but it struck me how quickly your circumstances can change out here, and how prepared you have to be.

Next I forced myself to eat something. I wasn't hungry but I knew that I had to give my body the energy it needed to continue, so I forced down a tuna and pasta mix, and then some sugar lollies. The tuna and pasta would give me some slow-release energy, while the lollies would give me the instant burst that I so desperately needed.

I realised that everything up to this point had been relatively easy. Now things were getting real. I had a proper challenge in front of me.

I heard the faint hum of a vehicle and I got up to have a look. A four-wheel drive was approaching from the north. I thought I'd better at least put my riding pants back on. It was a white Mitsubishi Triton with two blokes inside, and they pulled up in front of me. They could both see the condition I was in—sweating, red and puffing—and immediately offered me water and food. I thanked them and said I had it covered, but it was nice of them to offer.

The driver told me he was a nurse, and that a few days previously he'd had to use his skills after an accident occurred further north on the CSR in the dune country. A vehicle had got bogged near the crest of a dune, and while the occupant was trying to unbog it, another vehicle travelling from the opposite direction had crested the same dune and collided with the bogged vehicle. Emergency services had been notified, but due to the isolated location help wasn't available for at least two days. One person had died.

The guys warned me of the hazards of that area, which I would soon be going through, and how the four-wheel drives had created run-up tracks and were hitting the dunes at crazy speeds instead of crawling over them slowly. I would have to be alert for oncoming traffic, they said.

This made me even more cautious. If the four-wheel drives were cresting at speed, and I needed speed to crest as well, this could be a recipe for disaster. I vowed to not forget this piece of advice.

It was only when I heard this story that I really understood how remote I was. The peace of mind I'd enjoyed knowing I had a personal locator beacon (PLB) and Garmin SOS button was shattered, now that I knew even a helicopter rescue was at least two days away. My riding would have to take on a whole new style.

I did have my UHF radio turned on and was frequently calling ahead when I was atop the dunes, but I hadn't received any responses so I didn't know whether the signal was getting out far enough. I would continue to use it, hoping it would increase my chances of avoiding any oncoming traffic. In any case, I'd be a lot more cautious in the upcoming dune country.

I thanked the guys for the heads-up. They were quite sombre as a result of their involvement in the tragedy, and I could tell it had affected them. I greatly appreciated them stopping and telling me about the dangers ahead.

> *Met a couple of blokes in a Triton, one is a nurse, told me about the death up ahead on the track. Danger is real out here.*
>
> *Thursday, 3 August*

•

The CSR, like the French Line has about 900 sand dunes to cross, with the larger ones over 20 metres high. This is approaching the height of the Big Red sand dune in the Simpson Desert, Australia's tallest sand dune. I guessed I was about a third of the way through them, but the bigger ones were still ahead.

It was hard to get going again after the exhaustion and with the knowledge I'd gained, but I got back into the saddle and rode off, albeit at a more cautious pace. The dune section was, as expected, twisty and deep, with the midday temperatures making the sand softer, and therefore harder to ride.

I started seeing the run-up tracks made by the four-wheel drives, and shivered at the thought of meeting one of those two-tonne monsters cresting at speed. To minimise the chances of a collision, I made sure that I never crested a dune in the centre line: I would always ride to the far left when approaching the top so I could spear off into the bush if an oncoming vehicle emerged. I always stood up when hitting the dunes, hoping I would spot the tall sand flags vehicles had attached to them, which might give me a little time to react.

I only saw a couple of four-wheel drives in this section, and thankfully not at the crests. I rode as hard as I could to clear the toughest part of the section by late afternoon, before stopping near Well 28 for an afternoon break.

There was an interesting little cave near where I stopped, so I walked up to it to have a look. But I was simply too tired to wander around and explore. Again, I plonked myself down under a shady tree to recuperate. I was buggered.

The country around me was changing. It had flattened out more, with low-lying saltbush and spinifex bordering the twin track, thickening here and there, with some slappy sticks thrown in occasionally for good measure. It was relentless: I'd get through the deep sand, only to be confronted by slappy sticks … I'd get past them and be confronted by sharp rocks … I'd get through them and be buried in more deep sand.

The Canning was wearing me down fast. I had at least another two days on it, so I had to get my mind in order and stay hard to continue. I had been making good time and was ahead of my planned schedule, which pleased me, but I was starting to think about getting off this damn track.

It was around 4pm, so there were a few more hours of daylight left. The air was cooling down so I was coming into prime riding time. I had to push myself and get going again.

I rode until about 6pm, pushing as hard as I could, and I had nothing left in the tank when I stopped. I couldn't go any further, my concentration was lapsing and I knew a fall wasn't far away if I continued. But I was pleased, I'd made it through the tough dune section without accident, and both the bike and I were unscathed. My exhausted arms felt like lead pipes, my hands barely able to hold the handlebars any longer.

I found a large, open gravel plain and pulled in, knowing this was me for the night. The ground was covered in the small red ironstone rocks I'd become used to riding on, but there were a few small and flat clay sections.

I found one that was big enough for my tent and set up there. It was as hard as concrete, and I had a bugger of a time getting my lightweight tent pegs into the ground. I bent several when I was hitting them with a rock, and skinned a knuckle in the process.

It's fair to say I wasn't a happy camper that night. But I had travelled over 340 kilometres today, across some of the hardest terrain I'd ever faced. Most importantly, I'd now crossed my eighth desert.

Ride notes—DEEP sand, French Line, twisted dunes. Exhausted by lunch. Blistered hand, cramping—knackered. Want to get as close to Kunawarritji as possible. ATTACK SAND—ROLL OVER rocks. Finished around 6pm, couldn't hold onto handlebars any longer, exhausted. Nearly fell off bike when stopped. Used a small amount of water from bladder for shower & cool down. Lay down on tarp panting like a dog! Covered 340 something kays today so big ride. About 120 kilometres out of Kunawarritji. Water from now on will be a real thing, going to fill both bladders and bottles, 19 litres in total. Sand riding is hard & dehydrated me again today, even though I was sucking on CamelBak. Water is a real worry. Rode to my limit today, all I can do is more hours & more distance. Cannot ride any faster, too rough and too dangerous. Slappy sticks smack me constantly—ride on the left to protect the oil cooler. Max speed there about 30 kph. Open sand country, fifth gear, 60–70 kph depending on corrugations. Bike constantly skating. Controllable, just. Fuck, it's hard. Passed a few four-wheel drives in the dunes—they use a run-up track & deeply scallop the face out. DR gets up easily! This is the most exhausted I've felt, but I can start to feel the finish which urges me on. Get to Kuna, then Billiluna & Tanami! Buggered, going to bed.

Thursday, 3 August

17

Confidence

4 August

My northward trek on the Canning Stock Route continued today with another small detour to refuel. I would be riding in the Great Sandy Desert aiming to cover as much distance as I could.

From the time my head hit my small inflatable pillow the night before, I didn't stir until I woke at sunrise. My body needed a solid rest to recuperate from the previous day's exertions, and to prepare itself for another day of the same punishment. Funnily enough, though, the first thought that popped into my head when I woke up was, *I'm going to get another iced coffee today at Kunawarritji.* It's the little things that matter!

> Nice camp overnight, cool breeze into the tent. Circulated the air so I could smell myself—disgusting! Woke early—no coffee, just porridge, worried about dehydration in the dunes.
>
> Friday, 4 August

The morning was crisp, as it always is out in the desert at this time of year. I was up before dawn, packed up and was thumbing the starter just as the sun was rising on the horizon. I wanted to maximise my time riding in the cool morning air, when the sand was at its firmest.

As the track was weaving north, the rising sun from the east cast long shadows across it from the low-level spinifex shrubbery at the sides. This made the surface very hard to read. I couldn't judge the sand depth or contrast well, so I ended up riding much slower than I normally would have. Maybe the early start wasn't worth it after all.

The track started in the usual way, twin wheel tracks, corrugated deep sand ruts, with slappy sticks lining each side. It fluctuated between this and open sections of high-speed sand corrugations. After about 30 minutes of constant vibrations, my hands and wrists started playing up—and then, not long after, my right hand went numb. It had been doing this on and off for the previous two days, and there was nothing I could do about it apart from taking it off the handlebars when I could and trying to get the blood flowing again. It was starting to take a toll.

Along with the numbness I was feeling, I was also starting to contend with blisters on the palms of my hands around the base of my fingers. They had initially started to callus up, but in parts the skin was rubbed red raw from the constant vibrations of the corrugations. The Canning was finding every weakness in my body and making me pay for every kilometre I travelled.

A huge amount of regrowth on this section of the CSR had occurred over the previous two years, when the track had been closed. The four-wheel drives had done a good job of clearing the way by bulldozing through, but they'd left debris all over the track. Snapped branches, in particular, had sharp ends that were ready to spear into my skin or saddlebags, and it was a constant battle to avoid them. Due to the heat, I was only wearing a singlet, a mesh body armour suit and a riding jersey, and the little forearm protection I had would not protect me if I brushed too close to the branches. Sharp sticks on the ground in the centre of the track also had to be avoided as much as possible, to minimise the chances of a puncture. So it was a constant battle avoiding the worst in the centre and at the sides.

It was around the Well 32 area that I made my first navigation error of the trip. Because of vegetation regrowth and flooding earlier in the year, a lot of the original track had been overgrown or bypassed due to damage, meaning there were numerous side tracks leading to the wells. Not all of these were on my GPS map. Some headed in the right direction but didn't follow the same path; others, as I was soon to find out, didn't.

I took one of these tracks leading out from a well, only for it to turn into a deep, sandy dead end after about 500 metres. The track got narrower and narrower, with slappy sticks eventually overgrowing the entire track, making it impassable. I knew then that I'd gone the wrong way and had to turn around, but I had little room in which to do so.

Turning a heavy bike around in a tight space is a challenge; doing it in deep sand adds a whole new level of difficulty. I tried to do a donut—turning the handlebars sharply to one side and spinning the rear wheel so the bike tracks around in a small circle—but that didn't work due to the bike's weight, and I dropped it in the sand. I had been huffing and puffing up to that point, dog-paddling through the deep sand, and was pretty knackered already, but I had to find some more energy to pick up the bike.

There is a technique for picking up a heavy bike, and I followed it to the letter. I turned the handlebar touching the ground backwards, so it was tucked under the tank as much as possible, then squatted down with my back to the bike. I grabbed the handlebar with my hands behind my back and drove straight up with my legs, trying to stand up from the squatting position.

That makes it sound easy, but it wasn't. I was sweating, grunting and groaning—not a pretty sight! The bike and I squirmed around in the sand and it wasn't easy at all. Eventually, I got the bike nearly upright, then I walked back a step or so to get it vertical before I turned around. I kicked the sidestand down, my chest heaving, and rested until I got my breath back.

In situations like this, you can always lighten the bike by unloading it first. But I didn't want the hassle of doing this, as I would have lost even more time. I had trained and practised for these types of situations, and knew I had the strength to lift the bike fully loaded. It took everything I had but I got it done. However, I knew that if I dropped the bike again soon, it might be a different outcome!

So, there I was, covered in sweat again, and it was only 8.30 in the morning! I had expended more energy than I had wanted to by this time of day, so I vowed to conserve my energy when I could.

I backtracked to where I'd turned off and stopped at the well for a bit, then I scouted around looking at the different track options. I saw another track that appeared to be heading in the right direction and was well used, with fresh wheel tracks, so I took it. I followed it for about a kilometre before stopping to check my GPS map. It confirmed I was heading in the right direction. Now it was full steam ahead to Kunawarritji.

Was fatigued early on, took a wrong turn (tracks everywhere), tried to do a U-turn and dropped bike in deep sand. Took all my energy to lift it. Sat there huffing for ten minutes.

Tried to ride on but too exhausted, so stopped for a while under a shady tree to recover.

Friday, 4 August

•

Kunawarritji, sometimes known as Well 33, is the main Indigenous community on the CSR that is used by all travellers. It's roughly halfway between Wiluna and Billiluna, so all the four-wheel drivers make it their main resupply point. Kunawarritji has a population of under 100 people and was established in the early 1980s by a group of local Martu people from the nearby community of Punmu. There are both diesel and Opal fuel supplies available, a well-stocked minimart and accommodation options if you want to stay there. It was another oasis in the desert for me.

It was around 9.30am that I reached Kunawarritji and I headed straight to the self-service fuel pumps, where I filled up my main tank and my fuel bladder. Most of the communities nowadays have 24-hour fuel pumps that take credit cards, which eliminates the worry about whether or not you'll be able to get fuel on any given day. It was about 700 kilometres to Billiluna, so my main tank would almost get me there alone, but I wanted a reserve fuel capacity just in case. I wasn't about to break my golden rule. I knew there would be a weight penalty, but I would just have to manage it.

From the fuel pumps it was a short ride to the centre of town, where the shop and accommodation were situated. As I pulled up, a few locals who were hanging out in the nearby park gave me a nod, and I waved in return. They must have seen all sorts of people and all shapes and sizes of vehicles coming and going from their little town.

My next priority was water, so I headed straight into the shop and grabbed a few two-litre water bottles, enough to fill up all my bladders and bottles. Information about water quality in the remaining wells was limited, and I didn't want to rely on them anyway. I wouldn't be able to purchase water in Billiluna when I got there as the shop would be closed, so I wasn't sure where my next resupply would come from.

With everything filled to the brim, I had 19 litres of water onboard. And with the additional 44 litres of fuel, the bike was sitting down low again. Even with its beefed-up suspension, you could still see it was carrying a very heavy load. This would mean riding a wallowing whale for the rest of the day. There was no other choice, though. Sure, I could have skimped on water, and taken on less fuel, but we were only talking about a few kilograms here and there.

Safety was at the forefront of my mind when I was preparing to head back out to the CSR. I wanted at least two days' worth in reserve in case I became stranded or wasn't able to top up. I'm not the type of guy who just says, 'She'll be right,' or who is willing to rely on passing four-wheel drives for help. This was a totally self-sufficient mission I was on. I also made sure to down an iced coffee while I was there!

In the shop, I had a chat with the manager, who was serving at the register, and got talking to him about my trip and what I was trying to achieve. He was polite enough but I got the feeling he'd heard all kinds of stories from all kinds of travellers coming through here before, and that a lot of those dreams had never been realised due to breakdowns and other misfortunes. The outback is an unforgiving place, as he knew only too well.

He told me about a husband-and-wife team who had come up from Wiluna on a couple of motorbikes a couple of weeks prior, and ended up staying in Kunawarritji for a few days. Apparently, the corrugations were too much for them and their hands and arms couldn't take any more, so they checked into the accommodation to rest their hands before turning off the CSR.

I could empathise with them—I literally felt their pain!—but for me there was no stopping or turning off.

I walked around my bike, visually inspecting everything, looking for damage, cracks or other issues before I left. This would be the only place I could get repairs done if they were needed, so I had to be certain that the bike was up to another two or so days of punishment. Satisfied that everything was okay, I headed back out onto the Canning.

•

The heat was building up now, and I sucked on my CamelBak to stay hydrated as I travelled further north and closer to the end of the CSR. It wasn't long before I reached another well and found a ton of bypass tracks going in all directions. I picked what I thought was the right one and headed off in that direction.

The track looked reasonably well used, which was something I looked for when choosing a track to follow as it was usually a good indicator. I continued along in that direction for about a kilometre, but I began noticing that it was turning in what I thought was no longer a northerly heading. Having ridden the worst tracks imaginable, it was hard to determine whether this was just another shitty track on the Canning or an offshoot.

I stopped to check the GPS and, sure enough, this track had me heading due east instead of north and had moved me off the main Canning Stock Route. This track went to God knows where, so I had to turn around and head back.

At the well I did as I had done before, checking the GPS and riding around searching for the best used track that seemed to head in the right direction. I picked a different one and rode it for about 500 metres before checking my GPS location. This time I was going the right way, so I continued on.

My map was telling me that I was soon due to cross into the Great Sandy Desert, the ninth desert of my ten-desert Guinness World Record attempt. That meant I had to keep a lookout for other travellers who could witness my traversing this part of the Canning Stock Route.

Now the country opened up again. The dunes were more spaced out, which allowed me to look around a little more. There were always remnants of previous travellers' mishaps, mostly in the shape of wrecked and rusting four-wheel drives of all shapes and sizes, but this time I saw a relic of a different kind. It was an old rusty motorcycle frame that had obviously been there for quite a few years. I didn't know what type of bike it was, or what had happened to the rider, but it seemed like an omen of sorts—a warning that bikes were not immune to the harshness of the Canning.

I pushed on, enjoying the slight reprieve from the hardcore sand dunes as the country firmed up a little, moving back into the reddish ironstone country that I'd encountered earlier on.

Hot and tired at Pierre Springs, Canning Stock Route.

Near Terrace Hill, Canning Stock Route.

Windy Corner, Talawana Track.

Exhausted near Well 28, Canning Stock Route.

Camping on the Canning Stock Route. The desert evenings in the remoteness of Central Australia are stunning.

The track to nowhere—Canning Stock Route near Well 32, Gibson Desert.

Well 41, 'Tiru',
Canning Stock Route.

Sand dunes in between Well 43 and Well 44, Canning Stock Route. They were fun, fast and straight!

Gravity Lakes, Canning Stock Route. These are a series of small claypans that fill up and hold water after rain. The pink colour comes from a pigment released from the bacteria that's present in the water.

Slappy sticks, northern Canning Stock Route. These are the tree branches that grow right to the side of the wheel tracks on which I was riding. The branches constantly slap the bike and your arm gets whipped and will end up quite badly bruised.

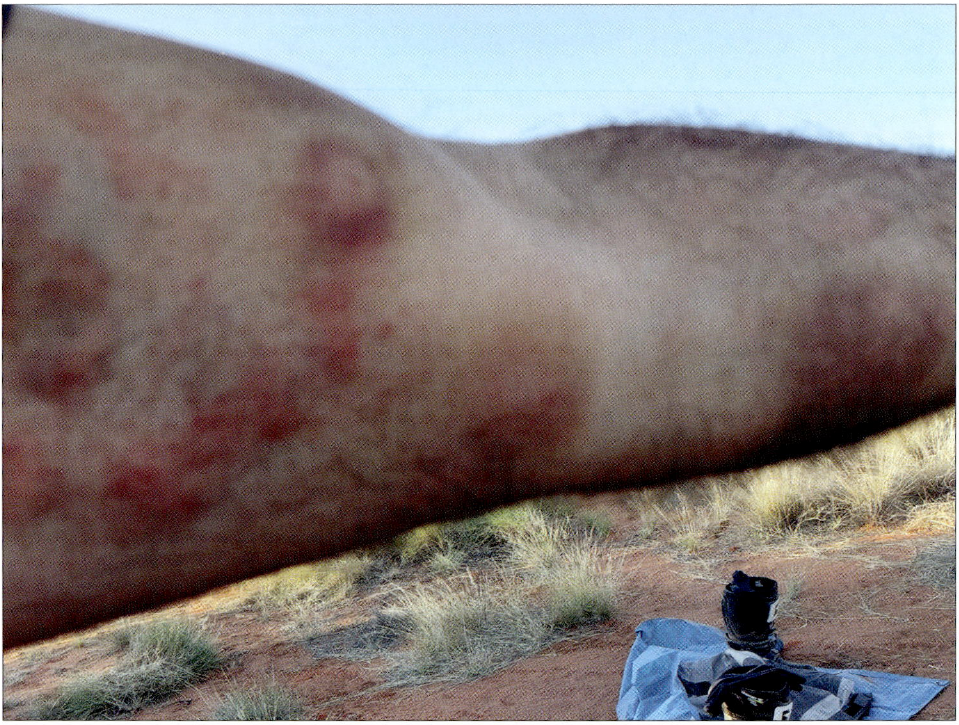

The welts caused by slappy sticks. Trust me, it's painful!

Breaden Hills meeting with Tony and his wife Lynda. *Tony Mahood*

On the home stretch, Tanami Road, Tanami Desert.

At the finish line! Yuendumu Big Shop, Northern Territory.

A new Guinness World Record. The fastest time to cross all ten Australian deserts on motorbike unsupported: 14 days, 2 hours and 12 minutes.

Back home with my Suzuki DR650 that took me across Australia's ten deserts in just a fortnight. This humble but tough machine performed outstandingly in the most difficult of conditions and was an indispensable part of my Guinness World Record–breaking ride. *AJ Nitz Images*

It felt good to have a hard surface under my tyres again. It was early in the afternoon when I spotted the first vehicles I'd seen all day: a convoy of two four-wheel drives travelling south. I pulled over to the left-hand side of the track, allowing them to pull up to me. It was there that I met Dick and his wife, Lynn.

As soon as I started talking to Dick, I knew he was a rider too, and it turned out that he had previously ridden the Canning. Within about five minutes, we had worked out that we were both part of an online motorcycle forum for adventure motorcycle riders. In fact, I recalled reading his ride report from 2015, when he and two of his mates rode south from Billiluna to Wiluna, with Dick on his KTM 640. Talk about a small world! I told Dick I'd pored over his ride report as part of my research for the trip, and thanked him for the detail he'd put in it. Unfortunately, Dick's ride had finished prematurely, when one of his group's riders had to be driven out in a passing four-wheel drive after sustaining a leg injury.

This time, Dick and Lynn were doing the CSR in the luxury of their four-wheel drive. They had left Victoria and travelled up to Curtin Springs, on the Oodnadatta Track in South Australia, and from there had done the tour of Kings Canyon to Alice Springs and onto the Tanami Road. They'd left the relative comforts of Billiluna a few days before we met, and they were going to take another two weeks or so to do the rest of the Canning.

It was great meeting the man behind the ride report, and putting a face to a name. Dick kindly witnessed my crossing of the Great Sandy Desert—another one ticked off my list. I was quite happy spending some time chatting with Dick and Lynn, and if I'd been in different circumstances I'm sure we would have shared a few beers and a few more yarns. But not this time. I had distance to cover, and they would be soon looking for a campsite, so I thanked them and we parted ways.

•

I saw on my GPS that I was approaching Tobin Lake. It also showed a number of campsites around Well 39, just prior to the lake's edge, and I thought that would be a good place to pull up for the night. If the map was right, the next day would be an easy start on some firmer ground around the lake. I looked forward to that.

Tobin Lake was named after Michael Tobin, an original member of Alfred Canning's 1906 expedition along the stock route. Tobin was fatally speared by a local Indigenous person during this trek and killed; his grave lies north of the lake named after him, near Well 40. The gravesite is a point of interest for tourists along the Canning, but I was not planning on stopping there. It was a detour off the main track and I didn't want to risk any side trips.

It was dusk by the time I selected a campsite and pulled over. Again I was exhausted. It had been another tiring day of riding, and I'd pushed myself to my limits. I could feel my riding pants were getting looser. I was closer to my goal tonight, though, which felt good. Almost for the first time, I was sure that the Guinness World Record was within my grasp.

I set up camp in quick time. There was no messing about; by now I was a well-oiled machine. Everything was soon in its place and I was sitting down and sipping on a caramel latte generously laced with condensed milk.

I felt like chatting and exchanged messages with my family and friends. Tonight was an unusual night for me in that even though

I was physically drained, I felt emotionally strong. I was into my ninth desert and had covered about 275 hard kilometres today. I received messages of support from everyone and had a great night in the bush, all on my own but connected to my supporters.

> Left too early this morning, before 7, hard riding so early, sun in face & shadows on road. Cannot read sand depth or contrast—dangerous. Made Kuna about 9.30am. Filled all fuel and water—19 litres, unsure about wells. Using nearly five litres of water a day, can't suck it in fast enough. Was fatigued again, sand roads had me skating around at 60–70 kph, brutal on hands and wrists.
>
> Rode on to about 6.30pm, coincided with a campsite just north of Well 39. Did about 275 kilometres today, happy with that. I know what the CSR is now, relentless sand dunes, slappy sticks, corrugations. Started to feel the end & confident in my ability to get through it all. Will look for water tomorrow, Well 41 apparently has good water, as well as 46 and 49. So if I can make Well 46 or Well 49, can have a shower!
>
> Friday, 4 August

18

Battered and Bruised

5 August

Today would be more of the same, continue north on the Canning Stock Route while I passed through the Great Sandy Desert. There was no real plan, just cover as much distance as I could and hopefully end up at a well with a water supply as an overnight campsite.

I was five days ahead of schedule now. I was covering a lot more ground each day than I had the previous year with Farmer. When riding solo, I found, I always seemed to push myself a bit more.

While sipping my morning coffee, I looked at my bike in amazement. It was soaking up so much punishment, day after day after day. It looked like it was in a sorry state—the salt water from Lake Disappointment had started rusting the chain, the sprockets, the frame rails and the exhaust. It was also covered in red dust and mud, and parts of it were held together with cable ties. Yet I felt a real connection with it out here: I had to look after it in order for it to look after me.

To make our life a little easier, I emptied the last fuel bladder into the main tank, which reduced the weight on the rear of the bike. That would dramatically improve the handling when I got going today. I also shuffled my water containers around to ensure the weight was distributed evenly on both sides, and as low as possible. I wasn't sure how hard the riding was going to be today but I wanted to have the bike set up as well as possible.

As I had expected, the start of the day's riding was a lot easier as I neared Tobin Lake, with the sand making way for a firm clay base that was awesome to ride on. There was a good 20 kilometres or so of this terrain as I skirted the lakebed, which helped get me warmed up for the punishment ahead.

I rode past the turnoff to Tobin's gravesite, sparing a thought for what it must have been like out here in 1906 with none of the technology that we now enjoy. The explorers might as well have been on another planet. Tough times indeed.

After Tobin Lake, the track returned to its original state of twin sand ruts and slappy sticks. On this particular morning, they caught me out. My speed was down due to the proximity of the branches to the side of the track: they were really close and constantly hitting my handlebars hard, causing me to strain to keep the bike straight. I wasn't able to ride the centre line due to the vegetation, so was forced to ride on the right side of the left wheel rut to avoid them as much as possible. My front wheel was constantly biting at the edge of the left-hand sand rut, and for a while the steering damper was doing a good job of keeping the bike straight.

At one moment, though, the front wheel bit hard and slid out, causing me and the bike to go down. Luckily, I was only riding in first gear and at slow speed, so it was more of a step-off than a fall, but it was frustrating to have to expend more energy picking the bike up, dusting myself off and getting on again. I had no rhythm riding through this sort of terrain—there was no respite. It was fatiguing. I could feel my energy draining away and committed to concentrate harder.

It was a constant battle all the way to Well 41, some 80 kilometres away. I was constantly in first and second gear, ploughing through the soft sand and getting whipped by slappy sticks. My left arm was really hurting from the constant punishment.

At one stage, a branch speared under the peak of my helmet, nearly tearing it off. Fortunately, I had my visor down, but it damaged the peak nonetheless. *Better to damage my helmet than lose an eye*, I reflected. *Note to self: always keep my visor down in the slappy sticks, no matter how hot I get!* The broken helmet peak was easily fixed, with some more cable ties coming to the rescue.

At this stage of the morning, I was not having a good time. Well 41 was a slight turn off the main track, and the country opened up around it. It was a welcome sight and served as my morning tea stop.

The well had been restored and was in good shape, so I opened the metal covers, dropped the pail in and drew up some water. It was clean enough but stained brown; that could have been caused by a number of natural causes, but I still wasn't going to drink it. If you were in need, I supposed, it could be made usable with filtration and boiling. I couldn't see any dead animals in it, so I poured it over my head and had a wash. Damn, did that feel good!

The Canning continued northwards, weaving between some more dry lakes. It wasn't until I got up to near Guli Lake that I saw my first camel on the CSR. It was out in the scrub, a couple of hundred metres off the track, so I stopped to have a look. It appeared to be a solitary animal, and it reminded me of the fun times I'd had on the Anne Beadell Highway trying to pass that big bull. I didn't want a repeat of that. I wondered why I hadn't seen more camels along the CSR.

The track was a lot more open in this section, with low-lying spinifex grass and sand dunes about five metres tall. It was actually pleasant riding through this open country, and not too tiring. I had another look at the GPS and saw the sand ridge markings tightening up, which meant I would be looking at a lot more sand dunes pretty soon.

Sure enough, not long after the camel sighting the dunes reappeared. They gradually increased in size—the largest, I reckon, was at least 20 metres tall. The track wove around and through them at some stages, and it was quite fun when I could develop and maintain a rhythm across the sand, hitting the corners again like berms.

The majority had a decent straight run-up, which wasn't hard to get up and over, even on the steepest of them. The four-wheel drives had been here and the dune faces were deeply scalloped out, so the only safe way to deal with them efficiently was at speed. I would hit the dune faces in second or third gear and glide up to the top and over the softest part, then power down the other side to prevent the front wheel from bogging down.

There was about 100 kilometres of this roller-coaster through the dunes, and already I could feel the fatigue coming on. The dunes were spaced about two to four kilometres apart in this section and had been the tallest I'd encountered on the Canning. I'd hit them at midday and so I had no choice but to ride hard and get through them as fast as I could. I called out my location on the UHF radio when I could, but there were no vehicles responding so it seemed I was all alone out there.

I pushed hard, hitting 70 to 80 kph down the faces and across the corrugated twin track in between, then about 40 to 50 kph up the faces. Climbing the dune faces, cresting and then descending them was quite exhilarating when they all lined up straight. The bike did it easily and it was fun. The riding wasn't as physically demanding as it had been earlier this morning, and I relished the relative ease with which I was getting through it.

In the back of my mind, though, was what I'd heard from the fellas in the Mitsubishi Triton. I had to keep my speed in check, ride to the left wherever possible and scan as far ahead as I could. If the terrain stayed open like this, I would be making good distance today.

•

As the dunes petered out, the terrain changed again and I approached what looked like another body of water. I assumed it was another salt lake, but this time it was pink. A quick check of the GPS showed it to be Gravity Lakes. These are a series of small claypans that fill up and hold water after rain. Since there'd been a whole lot of rain over the preceding months, they were quite full. The pink colour came from a pigment released from the bacteria that's present in the water. It really was quite spectacular.

The track ahead of me seemed to lead straight into the body of water, and I wondered how firm the base was. I rode up to the edge and the claypan was still very firm where it was dry. The water didn't look very deep, and I thought how much fun it would be to zoom right across the shallow lake, spraying up plumes of what looked like strawberry milk.

But then I had a reality check. I wasn't just down the road from a bunch of mates who'd be ready to pull me out if I got stuck, so there would be no spraying strawberry milk around today. I backtracked a little to the edge of the body of water and followed it around to the other side, where I saw the track exited the claypan. I checked the GPS again to make sure it was the right way out and continued northwards.

The changing scenery and the diversity of plants and wildlife was amazing. The terrain was harsh and unforgiving, but beautiful too. It was awesome to see that body of water and know how much life it provided to the surrounding flora and fauna. In other times I would have taken a walk out into it, but not today.

The sand dunes subsided after Gravity Lakes and the country opened up a lot more, but it introduced another hazard—one I'd researched and heard about. It was also a hazard that had stopped a few previous riders dead in their tracks. Termite mounds.

These, in my opinion, are the most dangerous hazard for motorcycle riders along the Canning Stock Route. They vary in size, with the bigger ones, because they are visible, not being a problem. It's the smaller ones you can't see that are the issue. The track here was badly corrugated sandy twin wheel tracks which had thick spinifex grasses on either side, usually around 50 to 70 centimetres tall. Hidden among the spinifex, even right at the edge of the track, are the smaller termite mounds that can't be seen. They can rip your foot right off the footpeg if hit.

As soon as I spotted the first one, I adjusted my riding position immediately, moving the balls of my feet back on the footpegs and turning the front of my foot inwards, hugging the bike tightly at the ankles. I didn't want my feet pointed outward, as a termite mound strike could catch my foot and break my leg. I had seen pictures online of the carnage termite mounds had caused riders in this way.

This part of the ride was mentally tiring, fighting the bike to keep it away from the edge of the sandy track, scanning ahead for termite mounds, and constantly checking and adjusting my riding position. I couldn't relax at all. This was the only way I could prevent myself from becoming another casualty.

I kept alert and rode on until I saw the jagged outline of the Breaden Hills approaching. These were named after Joe Breaden, a member of David Carnegie's 1896–97 exploration party, the first Europeans to explore this part of the Great Sandy Desert. The Breaden Hills are a series of smallish ranges spread out in the northern section of the Canning and provide another change of scenery. Again, it never ceased to amaze me what I would see next out here. I slowed down a little to take in the views and snapped a few more pictures.

It was around this area that I spotted a vehicle camped up in front of one of the rocky outcrops, so I made my way over. It was early afternoon, so I thought I might as well have an afternoon snack and meet another traveller.

I introduced myself to Tony and his wife, Lynda, who had stopped here to camp overnight, unable to resist the beauty of the Breaden Hills area. They had travelled from Tasmania to complete the Canning Stock Route as part of a larger journey encompassing the Kimberley region of Western Australia and a Simpson Desert crossing. I told Tony about my Guinness World Record attempt and some of the deserts I'd passed through, and he agreed to be another witness for my crossing of the Great Sandy Desert.

As we were chatting, Lynda brought me out a fresh apple, which looked delicious. I was keen to have a bite but politely declined, explaining that I was attempting the record unsupported and it wouldn't be in the spirit of the challenge to accept anything, even an apple. We all had a chuckle about that.

The afternoon sun was reflecting the red ironstone off the hills around us and looked amazing. They had certainly picked a wonderful spot to camp for the night.

I checked the map while I was there and saw that it seemed possible to make Well 49 this afternoon. All the reports said there was good water there, and I wanted a shower! So I said my goodbyes, wished Tony and Lynda well for the rest of their journey and set off.

•

The Canning made me work hard to get to my final destination for the day. The track closed up again and the slappy sticks returned with a vengeance. By now my left arm was very sore—it had been whipped by branches for three or so days now, and was covered in purple bruises. Every time a branch whipped me I winced with pain. That, of course, made me jerk the handlebars, adding to the instability. I had to block all this out and stay hard again to push through. I was back to first and second gear again, but come hell or high water I was getting to Well 49 tonight!

There was about 35 kilometres of this before Well 49 appeared. I'd averaged less than 30 kph since I left Tony and Lynda, and it was all hard going. Both bike and rider were battered and bruised. I didn't know how much longer I could do this.

I wasn't the only traveller to take advantage of the good water at Well 49. There was a large group of blokes from Kalgoorlie, who had been camped up there since late afternoon and had been on the beers. They were a rowdy bunch, but kindly offered me a cold one. I got a couple of funny looks when I said no to the beer and tried to explain why. Anyway, they were having a good time but all I wanted to do was sleep, so I set up my camp far enough away to not be disturbed and began to organise my things before it got too dark.

Well 49 also being Ranger Station had good quality tank water which was suitable for drinking so I took the opportunity to fill my six-litre water bladder and have a shower. It felt great, and perhaps washed some of the body odour off me. However, when I got back into my tent and crawled into my smelly sleeping bag, I'm sure I smelled the same again—but I didn't care.

I was now nearing the northern edge of the Great Sandy Desert, desert number nine. I'd travelled more than my planned distance again today, covering nearly another 350 kilometres on some pretty horrible tracks. But the end was now firmly in sight. Just the Tanami Desert left, one more day, I reckoned, and I'd have the record.

Immediately I cautioned myself to stop thinking like that—counting your chickens before they hatch is how accidents happen. I still had to take it one day at a time and not get ahead of myself. Yet I couldn't deny that the excitement inside me was building.

Good start out, dry lakes then nice flowing dunes, got some good Km's up, then slappy sticks. The track is really overgrown, even the end of the dune section got a little overgrown & twisty. Slow-speed fall in deep sand. Very tiring & used energy picking up bike. Slappy sticks whipping my left arm constantly—very bruised now. I ride always in the LH wheel track or middle to protect oil cooler on the RHS of the bike. Constantly scanning how close the branches are, how thick—can I hit them & get through or will they spear me off the track? How deep is sand—can I ride in the middle? Always scanning & assessing—very tiring. Add corrugations & you have to ride them fast but not too fast if you hit a slappy stick. Then come the leg breakers. A couple of riders have come unstuck by the termite mounds that are right next to the track. What else?

- Corrugations
- Deep sand
- Slappy sticks
- Termite mounds

Can it get any worse?!

Ended up making it to Well 49—fresh water & bush shower—nice group of guys from Kalgoorlie area camped up. They'd been on the cans all afternoon, nice enough. Didn't stay chatting for too long. Fell asleep in tent knackered and slept well.

Saturday, 5 August

19

Had Enough

6 August

I WOULD LEAVE THE GREAT SANDY DESERT TODAY AND MOVE INTO the Tanami Desert, the last of the ten Australian deserts I needed to cross. The finish line of Yuendumu was in sight, I didn't know whether it was achievable today, but I was going to give it a good crack.

This morning was the earliest I had got up for the whole trip. The sun hadn't even risen when I crawled out of my tent into the pre-dawn darkness. My mates from Kalgoorlie hadn't stirred, and not even the birds had started chirping. I'd rested well, but I'd had enough of the Canning Stock Route and I wanted to get off it—today!

I'd forgotten how hard it was riding at dawn with the sun in my eyes. I had to endure this again today as I left Well 49, with the first glimmers of sunlight breaching the horizon. I was focused and excited to be approaching the end of this hard track; the promise of smoother roads ahead really spurred me on.

But the Canning wasn't finished with me yet. The slappy sticks closed in again and started whipping my left arm, as if to give me one last reminder of how harsh it was out here. I flinched every time a branch struck my arm—I really was over it.

It was slow going, with deep, sandy ruts waiting to grab my front wheel, sunlight directly in my eyes and branches grabbing at my handlebars, so I was often down to first gear again, dog-paddling. I yelled out in my helmet in frustration several times as I ploughed through at a snail's pace, unable to gain any speed or rhythm. Even so, I was determined not to stop.

My inner voice kept repeating, *Stay hard*. It didn't matter what the track threw at me, I was approaching the end and I knew there was a better road ahead. My bike was in good shape, so I didn't stop. I pushed on and on—nothing was going to stop me from reaching the township of Billiluna marking the end of my journey along the Canning Stock Route.

I could see on my topographical map that the sand dune markings were thinning out, meaning the ground would be firming up. There was another salt lake system ahead of me, which was good news. Lake Gregory runs parallel to the Canning for about 20 kilometres, which would provide some respite once I got out of this thick scrub.

I bashed through the slappy sticks for what seemed an eternity, but I got through. I didn't know it at the time but that was the last time I would see them.

The lake system appeared, and like magic the country opened up again. I picked up speed on the firm clay and had a hoot in the cool morning air. Then the track led into farmland, and I started to see mobs of cattle and cattle grates. I was getting closer to civilisation again now.

This was a fun part of the ride and my spirits were high. I cruised along the farm track feeling super happy with myself, knowing I'd got through the worst of it. It continued like this for a couple of hours and I wove in and out of paddocks full of stock, over cattle grates and onto a wider dirt road. I now knew I'd made it through the worst the Canning could throw at me. I'd come through relatively unscathed—but I couldn't be sure until I made it to the next town.

I arrived in Billiluna around midmorning, and what a sight it was. I was so happy to be here. It felt like forever since I'd been in civilisation, and just seeing the buildings and houses made me feel part of the world again, even though it was Sunday and the shop was closed. I'd conquered the Canning Stock Route unsupported on a motorcycle—which in itself was a major feat of endurance—and I'd also achieved my longstanding personal goal of riding it. I felt great relief, as I knew what lay ahead having previously ridden through the Tanami Desert, and how much easier the riding would be, compared to what I'd just been through.

Billiluna, which is also known by its Indigenous names of Mindibungu and Kururrungku, is an isolated community in the Tanami Desert. It's approximately 175 kilometres from Halls Creek to the north and about 600 kilometres to Yuendumu to the south-east, and is one of only three fuel stops along the 1000 kilometres of the Tanami Road that I was about to travel. It's also the jumping-off point for travellers heading south on the Canning, so it's quite a busy hub in the winter months.

I had a few things to take care of before I could rest, though, so I got straight into it. My first task was to refuel at the 24-hour fuel bowsers, where I took on 38.5 litres. My next fuel stop would be at Yuendumu, at the eastern end of the Tanami Desert, my finish line. Then I removed the 14-tooth front sprocket, replacing it with a 15-tooth sprocket that would provide me with a higher top speed. After the battering the bike had taken, I gave it another good look over in anticipation for the rest of the day's cruising at higher speeds. There was not a thing out of place—all was in order. This bike was tough!

After my jobs were done, I found a shady spot on the verandah of the shop and had a morning snack of some trail mix, a muesli bar and lollies. I wanted my energy levels back up for the next big push. It had taken me three and a half hours to cover the previous 150 kilometres of the Canning, and I was keen to see how far I could push to the finish line 600 kilometres away. I also took some time to reflect on where I'd ridden from, what I had already done and where I was. I was close to the finish now and I wanted to savour the moment and let it all sink in.

My first marker point was at the Western Australian and Northern Territory border, which I suspected might have been the finish line for the current record. I intended to make this my first stop and record my time there anyway, before proceeding with my original plan of finishing at Yuendumu.

I left Billiluna all smiles—I'd conquered the Canning Stock Route unsupported, which put me in an elite club of only a handful of motorcycle riders. Even if I didn't get the record, I would have been satisfied as this had been a big bucket list item for me. Leaving Billiluna, I turned to the right and was greeted by a spacious red-dirt road, some four to five lanes wide. This was the Tanami Road, which went more or less in a straight line all the way to Alice Springs, nearly 900 kilometres away.

It was mostly a south-east direction I would be travelling down, as I opened the throttle and accelerated up through the gears—even into fifth, which I hadn't used for quite a few days—until I reached my cruising speed of 100 kph. The wind was in my face, the sun was shining and life was good. Don't get me wrong, the Tanami Road is still a very rough and sandy corrugated dirt road for hundreds of kilometres, but compared to what I'd been through it felt like a freeway.

The Tanami Desert is a wide-open wilderness area, with low-lying spinifex grassland stretching off as far as the eye can see.

There are small sand ridges but nothing compared to where I'd been, along with areas of scrubland littered with mulga and acacia trees. It never ceased to amaze me how this country kept transitioning. It's a big, barren landscape, and made me feel insignificant as I rode through.

I watched as the kilometres ticked over on the odometer, then turned my mind to evidence again. I needed witnesses to prove I was now crossing desert number ten. After a while I crested a slight rise and saw a road train parked up on the side of the track. This was my chance.

I pulled up and walked over to the driver, whose name was Adam, and said g'day. Adam was driving a monstrous road train, carrying cattle between stations. It had four trailers attached behind the truck and was over 50 metres long—what a machine! I told him what I was doing and asked if he'd mind being a witness for me, and he agreed. With my tenth desert witnessed, I felt a bit more comfortable—now I only had to get myself to the finish line. I thanked Adam for being a part of my journey and then hit the track again.

Around lunchtime, I arrived at the border marker. There was nothing there but a big metal sign telling you where you are. The road was the same on either side, and the landscape didn't change either. Again I appreciated just how big Australia is.

I pulled up, took the obligatory photo and recorded my time. I used the chance to have some lunch, while thinking a little about whether this was the actual finishing line for the previous record. It didn't really matter to me, as my goal was already set. My finish line was now only 450 kilometres away. Could I make it today? I was sure going to try.

My backside was now just as sore as my hands and wrists, my riding gear was filthy, I stank and generally looked and felt pretty awful. I was now riding side saddle, only putting one butt cheek at a time on the seat, as well as slowing down and standing up every so often to relieve the pressure. I kept that up for kilometre after kilometre, hour after hour, for as long as I could. Then my shoulders started cramping from maintaining the one position for so long, which forced me to pull over every so often to stretch them out. My body was in bad shape.

With the consistent higher speeds, my concentration was working overtime as well, trying to pick the sand ridges when they appeared, the washouts and corrugations—everything was coming at me faster now. Many times I had to slow down so I could look off the track, changing my gaze to refocus my strained eyes and reset my concentration.

Along the way I came around a bend in the road to see a large cloud of dust up ahead. That could mean only one thing: a road train. I was moving faster than the dust cloud, though, and as I got closer it was clear that the truck was travelling in the same direction as me. I wondered if I was going to be able to get past.

As I got closer to the big rig, I used my UHF radio to broadcast my position, telling the truckie he had a bike behind him. The wind was blowing across the road, pushing all the dust to the right-hand side, right where I would have to drive if I overtook him. There was no way I was going to do that—the road train had four trailers on, and I'd be blind if I entered that billowing dust cloud.

Much to my delight, I got a reply on the radio, and slowly the truck and all its trailers moved across to the right-hand side of the road, which opened up a clear path for me on the left. I took advantage of the opportunity to pass and gunned the bike along the truck's left-hand side, giving him a big wave as I did. The size of these rumbling beasts is just enormous, and I was grateful to the driver for his thoughtfulness in making it possible for me to pass safely.

•

I was closing in on Yuendumu, but the afternoon sun was setting now and the Tanami Road was no place for a small dirt bike to be after dark. There were just too many road hazards, not to mention all the wildlife, that could bring me unstuck. I was definitely going to stick to my rule of not riding after dark. Before night fell, though, I was sure as hell going to use every last minute of the available daylight.

I could feel the energy draining from my body and fatigue setting in once again. Even though the road was in much better shape than I'd been used to, errors at this higher speed could be fatal, so I varied my speed, more to break the monotony, took a few more breaks to stretch and tried to look after myself. But I was too far from Yuendumu to reach it today—I had about 90 kilometres to go, I calculated—and the sun was setting fast. I needed to get off the road soon. In particular, I didn't fancy encountering another road train after dark.

There were plenty of turn-outs along the side of the road, so I just picked a gap in the scrub and rode off into the bush, far enough from the road that my camp wouldn't be seen. But it was a real effort setting things up tonight as my arms and legs just weren't cooperating.

My Garmin tracker had been beeping all day with messages. All my family and friends had been tracking my progress, and they'd seen how close I was coming to the finish line. When my camp was set up, I read and replied to all the messages of support. Doing so made me reflect on the journey I'd been on. All day I had been so focused on getting to Yuendumu—I'd ridden over 650 kilometres. I'd get there tomorrow, probably early.

It saddened me a little to know the adventure was coming to a close.

> Up very early, 5.30, keen to get the hell off the CSR. Had enough of it. First 20–30 km deep rutted corrugated sand, slappy sticks, sun in face. Slapping my bruised arm, swearing in helmet. 1st gear very angry. Took about 1.5 hours to get into more open country and put the foot down to Billiluna. Filled up, put big sprocket on & hit Tanami flat out. Mind you, the Tanami is a rough, sandy, corrugated road but compared to the CSR it's a freeway. Sat on 100 to the border, where I did photos and recorded time. Managed to grab a road train driver who had stopped checking his load to be my witness. Then 110 for as far as I could. Wanted to make Yuendumu, 450 km away, had about five hours riding time. Didn't quite make it, that's ok, about 650 km for the day. Will hit Yuendumu in the morning, then cruise into Alice Springs.
>
> Body aching—knees, bum, hands, wrists, neck, shoulders. Need a rest, sleep-in & fresh food. Everything is an effort at the moment. Funny, yunno first thing I look for after picking a camp spot is a big rock to hammer in the tent pegs.

Found a round metal pipe today, not ideal, kept slipping and I was swearing out of frustration & fatigue.

Bike's run flawlessly—no problems. Very confidence-inspiring.

I sit here smelling my own pong, feeling grubby but feel amazed at the country I've been through. Navigated without too many errors, managed my fuel and water range & rations.

That's enough, tired now, going to bed.

Sunday, 6 August

20

Record Day

7 August

It was an odd feeling this morning knowing that this would be my last camp. I'd grown so accustomed to my own company, and now I was heading to the finish line and back to civilisation. It would take some adjustment.

As much as I was sick of it, I savoured my powdered coffee and porridge, which had been a morning routine since day one. Eating the same thing at the same time, day after day, had become almost a ritual. I had developed a new, if temporary, lifestyle that was so different from my life back in Canberra. It was an adventurous lifestyle, and an exciting one, but all good things must come to an end.

I was feeling quite nostalgic as I packed up camp for the last time and got riding. I timed my departure so I would arrive at the Yuendumu Big Shop—the general store—right on opening. They were to be my witnesses at the finish line of my Guinness World Record attempt.

The ride to Yuendumu was unremarkable. I was still very sore, and after about ten minutes on the bike all my aches and pains came flooding back. I encountered a couple of road trains heading west, seeing their clouds of dust billowing in the distance way before I saw the trucks themselves. That gave me plenty of time to pull off the road before they passed. The dust cloud that followed each one would be blinding for ages; sometimes they also flicked up rocks and stones, so it was best to stay right out of their way.

Up ahead, I saw the most amazing sight: the road turned from red dirt to black tar! It had been tarred all the way from Alice Springs since I was last here, and I would soon be back on the blacktop. The turnoff to Yuendumu followed shortly after, and I turned the bike to the left and headed towards the community along the sealed road.

The bitumen road was amazing—I could fully relax my mind and riding position without worrying about the terrain ahead. It was such a relief. Then I started to see the familiar shapes of houses, which seemed to welcome me in. As I rode into town, I followed the main road, which eventually led me to the general store. I arrived at Yuendumu Big Shop just before opening time, keen to be their first customer for the day.

Shortly after I arrived, a white utility vehicle rolled up and out got Steve, the manager. I approached him and explained my situation, knowing it was not every day he'd come to work and be asked to witness the completion of a Guinness World Record. As I explained my story to him, I wondered how he would react and whether he would sign up to witness my finish. Thankfully, Steve happily agreed to help out, and he also found another staff member who kindly obliged as my second witness.

As Steve gave me back my pen, I realised that was it. I felt a huge surge of adrenaline—I'd done it! Not only had I finished my unsupported motorcycle ride across all ten of Australia's deserts, but I had cut the existing record of 29 days, 19 hours and 38 minutes in half! By more than half, actually: by my estimate, my time was 14 days and a number of hours. That would be determined by Guinness World Records. I was over the moon. I wanted to dance around and jump up and down and yell woo-hoo, but I didn't, as there was a bit of a crowd forming around me.

Word had spread among the morning shoppers, and it wasn't long before members of the community wanted to shake my hand and take pictures with me and my bike. It was pretty cool sharing my excitement with them. There were kids who wanted to sit on my bike, while their parents wanted to know where I'd come from and where I was going. A lot of them couldn't believe I'd just ridden nonstop through all ten Australian deserts and finished up in their little town.

Next my Garmin tracker started pinging, as messages of congratulations came in from family and friends—it was all quite awesome. I was riding a wave of emotion and accomplishment, and sharing my joy with others.

I allowed myself some time to take it all in and chat to the folks around me, but I couldn't stay forever. I'd arranged to fly Stace up to Alice Springs and we had a fancy hotel booked, so I was keen to move on.

I said my goodbyes to Yuendumu, knowing I would always have fond memories of the place. Then I hit the tar road into Alice Springs with a clear head. Now I was in holiday mode!

RECORD DAY!

What a feeling, sore again but encouraged knowing I had an easy ride into Yuendumu. Usual routine, pee, porridge & coffee, pack up & go. The Tanami is a major road train route—heard them rumbling along all night. Got going and as soon as I sat on bike my butt was killing me! Sitting side-saddle all day. Got into Yuendumu & rocked up to the Big Shop—met the manager and one of the staff, who witnessed my arrival and finish time. 14 days and something hours! Hooray.

So I felt kind of funny. I'd smashed the record, some of the locals were shaking my hand, and the Garmin cheer squad were pinging my phone, but I was like, 'thank god that's done!' It was hard, the pressure is off. A bit of a relief but I wasn't yahooing in my helmet. I guess because I was always quietly confident I'd beat the record.

Anyway, Guinness World Record attempt completed now—very pleased. I've been nervous, anxious, fatigued, sore, keen & excited, but holy moly, what a ride! I think my desert riding days are now over … maybe.

Monday, 7 August

21

King of the Desert

The ride into Alice Springs was a breeze, the road was bitumen all the way and I was off the clock, no longer worrying about the time. Lee Kernaghan was playing in my helmet, the sun was out, life was good. I took this time just cruising along to reflect on what I'd just completed. Part of me was a little sorry it was over, the other part of me was looking forward to a cold beer and a good steak!

Before leaving home Stace and I had arranged for her to fly up to Alice Springs to meet me at the end of my journey. I was days ahead of my planned schedule and she wouldn't be arriving until Friday, another four days away, as her flights couldn't be changed. Consequently, the accommodation we'd booked wasn't available yet either. We were both a little disappointed at not being able to see each other on the day, but equally excited at how quickly I completed the record attempt. We would see each other soon enough.

The next four days I used to relax and have a look around Alice Springs. I'd checked into another hotel and got myself cleaned up as best as I could. It was great to get out of my riding gear and be off the bike. I walked everywhere!

I spent a fair bit of time in the Alice Springs public library using their computers to collate the evidence I had gathered along the ride and submit it to Guinness World Records. As mentioned earlier, their guidelines are very stringent so I checked and double checked everything I was submitting for accuracy.

The four days passed quickly and before I knew it Friday was here. It was back on the bike and out to the airport to meet Stace. I watched as her plane landed and picked her out of the line of people walking to the terminal. She spotted me as she walked in and we met each other with a big hug and kiss. She was immediately taken aback at the weight I'd lost during the ride, and with my unkempt beard, scruffy hair, bruising on my arms and scars on my face from the slappy sticks I looked like a wild man!

That night we had a picnic dinner on the verandah of our accommodation adjacent to the sandy riverbed of the Todd River. I made sure to have all the delicacies we loved as well as an ample supply of cold beers to wash everything down. We talked for hours about my experiences during the ride and I read Stace all the diary entries I'd made. It was quite an emotional experience reliving and sharing my thoughts and feelings with Stace, which gave her a real insight to the challenges I had faced and overcome.

I let Stace know that her support was invaluable putting my mind at ease and allowing me to focus on the moment when I was out there in the bush. I have total confidence in her and her ability to manage things while I'm away, as has been the case so many times over the years. I wanted her to know this was a team effort and she played a big part in this achievement.

We had a week to spend in Alice Springs and surrounds, so we hired a four-wheel drive and set about exploring the sights. She had never been in this part of Australia before, so we ticked off the main items like Uluru, Kata Tjuta, and all the sights along the East and West MacDonnell ranges. We really enjoyed the time together and she even got to see her first wild camels.

By the time the next Friday came around we were both ready to head home. I had my bike packed up again for the ride back to Marree and that morning I saw Stace off in a cab back to the airport.

This last leg of my riding journey would take me through the Indigenous community of Finke, along the Oodnadatta Track to the Pink Roadhouse and on to my planned overnight stop of William

Creek about 750 kilometres away. I'd never ridden the leg from Alice Springs to Finke before, however the rest would be familiar territory.

Every year the town of Finke swells in size for the Finke Desert race, which is one of the toughest desert races in the country. Competitors on motorbikes and offroad buggies leave Finke on day one, racing the 220 kilometres to Alice Springs along a sandy desert track. Then on day two of the event the competitors do it all again in reverse. The lowest time determines the winners of each class.

To make things interesting I rode south from Alice Springs finding the Finke racetrack and followed it down to Finke. It was deep soft red sand for the most part, with plenty of twists and jumps along the way. I'd seen the race on television, and riding the track made me appreciate the skills of the competitors who race along there at speed. The DR650 is no race bike, and being weighed down as it was made for slow going along this stretch, but it was fun nonetheless and would give a new perspective for watching the race in the future.

I refuelled in Finke, not hanging around for long as I still had a long way to ride. The rest of the trip would be quite straightforward as the road was more maintained with a gravel surface making for easy riding. I briefly stopped at the Pink Roadhouse at Oodnadatta to top up with fuel and kept pushing on for William Creek, arriving late that afternoon.

There was no way I was going to be using my tent tonight and I had booked a donga in the caravan park opposite the William Creek Hotel. I was lucky I'd booked ahead, as there was a campdrafting and bronco-branding event on this weekend, and the town was full of people. Once I was cleaned up, I managed to get a seat at the bar for a cold beer and counter meal. Another good riding day down.

The next morning was a bit sad when I got on the bike, as I knew it would be the last riding day of this epic trip. The bike had become part of me: man and machine, day after day, something which I had grown very accustomed to. It was to be a short ride of only about 200 kilometres, and I rose early as I wanted to start the drive home from Marree today.

There was rain forecast today, closer to Marree than William Creek, but as long as it wasn't too heavy it wouldn't affect the dirt surface of the Oodnadatta Track too much. The skies were grey and it was a bit cooler, so I added an extra layer under my riding jacket before setting off.

Along the way to Marree the Oodnadatta Track passes Lake Eyre. I'd been past here a few times before, but this time on the smaller bike I was gamer to ride to the lake's edge and grab a couple of photos. Lake Eyre is stunning; white salt flats and the shimmer of water are such a contrast to the surrounding desert landscape.

About 50 kilometres from Marree it started raining. It wasn't heavy and didn't bother me at all, as the road surface was very dry and soaked up the raindrops without making it too slippery. So, I just continued on at a steady pace until just before lunchtime when I arrived back in town. I rode over to my vehicle and trailer which were parked where I had left them and began packing up.

There was not much left to do apart from loading up the bike on the trailer, getting changed and hitting the road again. As I left Marree, I imagined I'd never return, but I knew I'd thought that before.

•

It was Wednesday, 30 August 2023, and I'd been home for about a week when I heard a familiar *ding* on my phone alerting me to a new email. I saw it was an email from Guinness World Records that said:

> We are thrilled to inform you that your application for fastest time to cross all ten Australian deserts on motorbike has been successful and you are now the Guinness World Records Title Holder!

I took a pause and read it again. I'd done it—I was so pleased! The time waiting for my evidence to be accepted had been nerve wracking, and finally it had all paid off. I told Stace and the rest of my family, who all shared my excitement that night. My riding buddies of course wanted to celebrate as well, so we arranged to meet up at a local pub later in the week for a beer.

It was about 6pm on the Friday night when I walked up to the Royal Hotel and saw Ken, Claude, Mark and Clancy sitting outside. I was greeted with handshakes and congratulations all round, and the guys were really keen to hear about my adventure. No sooner had I sat down than Ken removed a bag from under the table. From the bag he took a plastic gold crown, which he promptly placed on my head, crowning me 'King of the Desert'. It was now official.

Acknowledgements

THIS ODYSSEY CONSUMED ME FOR A TWELVE-MONTH PERIOD OF my life, and I became obsessed with every little detail. This was not something I undertook alone; and had such a great bunch of people supporting and encouraging me who must also be acknowledged.

To my wife, Stace: thank you for putting up with my obsession, not only with this trip but with all things motorcycling, and for supporting me during all the ups and downs along the way.

To my late grandparents Richard and Dorothy, and mum, Lucille: thank you for kick-starting my obsession for motorcycling in the first place, and for giving me the freedom to pursue it.

To my daughter, Teej, Uncle Geoff and family, and in-laws: thank you for all your support and messages of encouragement during my ride. They were invaluable in keeping my spirits high.

To my riding buddies: you bunch really inspired me to ride my best. I knew I couldn't fail with you guys behind me, as I'd never live it down if I did!

And to Freda: thank you for your guidance through this writing project. Your knowledge and support helped shape my ideas and get them down on paper.

Technical data and statistics

I KNOW THERE WILL BE READERS WHO (LIKE ME) ARE INTERESTED in motorcycling gear, so here are the details of everything I used, plus info on how I set up my bike for this adventure. All products are commercially available, as required by Guinness World Records.

Motorcycle

2021 Suzuki DR650—White

Bike modifications

Front tyre:	Golden Tyre GT216AA 'fatty' 90/100-21 (lasted the entire journey with no punctures)
Rear tyre:	Motoz Rallz 130/80/17 (lasted the entire journey with no punctures)

Front suspension:	0.58kg fork springs, 10 weight fork oil with DFX fork valves
Rear suspension:	9kg spring, with shock revalve
Steering damper:	MSC Moto RM3
Handlebars:	ProTaper KX 7/8 High Bend and 25mm risers
Handguards:	Barkbusters VPS
Fuel tank:	Safari 36 litre
Seat:	Custom two-tone touring seat
Exhaust:	Barrett slip-on pipe
Windscreen:	Screens For Bikes light tint
Mirrors:	Folding enduro mirrors
Rear rack:	Scaggs Moto Designs
Tail tidy:	VSM fender eliminator
Pegs:	JNS lowered fat pegs
Bike control:	Stegz Pegz, Heavy Duty Desert King
Engine protection:	B&B Offroad countershaft case saver, clutch and ignition covers
Frame protection:	Acerbis frame guards
Gearing:	14/15-44

Accessories

Tank bag:	Giant Loop Diablo
Saddlebags:	Andy Strapz—Avduro
Roll bag:	Caribee 50 litre
Fuel bladders:	Liquid Containment 12 litre (×2)
Fuel containers:	Hünersdorff 2 litre (×2)

Communications, navigation and safety

GPS/UHF:	Garmin RINO 750
Bluetooth:	Sena SR10
Helmet comms:	Cardo Packtalk Bold
SATCOM/SOS:	Garmin inReach
PLB:	GME ACCUSAT

Camping equipment

Tent:	Zempire Atom
Sleeping bag:	Klymit KSB
Sleeping pad:	Sea to Summit Comfort Plus
Water bladders:	Sea to Summit Watercell 4 and 6 litre
Water containers:	Nalgene 1.5 litre (×4)
Cooking:	MSR PocketRocket stove and Macpac Heat Exchange Pot

Riding gear

Pants:	KLIM Traverse
Jacket:	KLIM Traverse
Jersey:	O'Neal Element vented
Gloves:	Dririder Rallycross Pro
Boots:	Gaerne Fastback Enduro
Helmet:	Arai XD-4
Armour:	Fox Baseframe with D30 inserts
Backpack:	CamelBak Mule 3-litre Mil Spec Crux

Statistics

Distance ridden:	5484.1 kilometres
Fuel used:	Approximately 315 litres
Consumption:	17.41km/L or 5.74L/100 km
Highest fuel cost:	$5 per litre

What broke

Windscreen support bracket—repaired with cable ties
Helmet visor—repaired with cable ties
Push-to-talk button—repaired with cable ties